Hacking
Money

How You Can Crack The Wealth Codes To Create Abundance

Mark E. Yegge

HACKING MONEY

This course-book was written for people who were never properly taught the basics of creating their own financial success. That should cover just about everyone because our school system, sadly, doesn't teach these essential skills.

Goal: To become an "Epic Millionaire" (defined within)

This publication is designed to provide accurate and authoritative information in regard to the subject matter covered. It is sold with the understanding that the publisher is not hereby engaged in rendering legal, accounting, financial, or other professional advice or service. If legal advice or other expert assistance is required, the services of a competent professional person should be sought.

This book and other materials are available at special discounts to use as premiums and sales promotions or for use in corporate training programs. For more information, please contact us through the following website:

www.HackingMoney.com

Library of Congress Cataloging-in-Publication Data:

Yegge, Mark E. 1965 –
Hacking Money: How You Can Crack The Wealth Codes To Create Abundance / Mark E. Yegge

ISBN: 978-0-9792094-3-7

This book is printed on acid-free paper.

Table Of Contents

CHAPTER 1:
INTRODUCTION

> *Every person is*
> *a millionaire*
> *at something.*
>
> Mark Gaye

INTRODUCTION TO HACKING MONEY

So you want to be a millionaire, or at least wealthy or wealthier? Really? Well then why aren't you already? Maybe it's probably because you haven't figured out the strategies, or made a plan, or maybe just haven't had the right things fall into place to make it all happen. Or maybe you just spend too much time doing things that take you away from putting you on the path to becoming a millionaire. Or maybe you aren't **being** the kind of person that can be a millionaire yet. It's OK - because today is the first day of the rest of your life!

(By the way, when I refer to "millionaire" I mean not only monetarily (what this book is about), but also a millionaire in every aspect of your life: your wealth, your health, your relationships, etc.).

[By the way, I am going to be pretty blunt in this book because it may be a time for you to make a change. You know, if you ALWAYS do what you've always done, you'll ALWAYS get what you've always gotten. So I am going to challenge you often in this book, and that may be just what you need.]

Well, if you want to become a millionaire, now is your chance; your real chance. But it's gonna take some work it's going to take some focus. It's going to take some energy, and it's gonna take some time. But so what? Most people don't just win the lottery and become millionaires, do they? If you think it's going to be easy to become a millionaire, that's probably why you're not a millionaire already. But it doesn't have to be hard either. We will explain inside.

Before we get too far down the road here, I don't want you to think that this is just another money course book, because it is much more than that. What you are about to experience is part of the structure for becoming a Full-Life Millionaire™: a millionaire not only in your finances, but your health, your wealth, your relationships and the other critical parts of your life. It's not all about the money because what good is money if the rest of your life sucks? So, while we will focus about 90% of this course work on money, it is with the conscious intention that we want to be millionaires in every part of our life – and money can just help that along.

When I grew up, possibly just like you, I didn't have money and I struggled to make ends meet. All the time I was watching on TV and reading in the newspaper how the rich and famous were living their lives. And I thought to myself "can't I have that?" and "if not why not?" and "if so, how?"

So I embarked on a plan. I began to study millionaires. I studied what made them tick. I studied how they thought and behaved. As I studied the strategies that they used in business and in their personal lives, I began to seek out mentors, heroes, and role models. And then, I started to build a plan. That's the same plan you're about to read about in this manual.

You see once I figured it out, I boiled it down into a formula. And since it's a formula, it is repeatable. I've also tried to make it really simple. I figure I've read around 8,000 books on success, personal development, business, finances, and a myriad of other subjects that helped me get to where I am. I'm not saying I've arrived at where I want

3

to end up, because there's always room for growth. But what I am saying is I've gotten to the point where I live a life that few people can live.

Today, I travel all over the world and "work" from wherever I am. So far it's 56 countries and counting. My goal is to get to a hundred in the next few years, not because I necessarily want to see 100 different countries, but because I grow so much as a person when I experience a new country, new place, a new people and a new culture. I'm a citizen of the world and that's the path I have chosen. It's not for everyone, but it's for me and it's for me right now, but of course it could change. And if it changes it will be my choice.

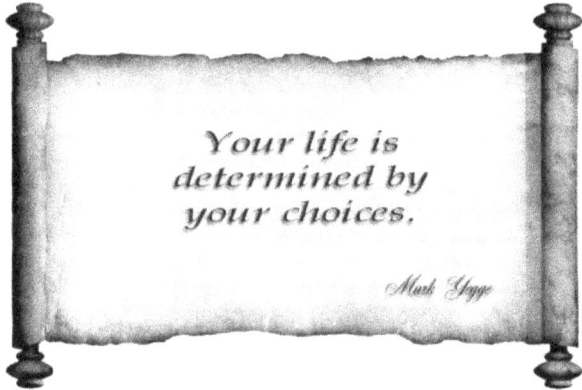

Your life is determined by your choices.

Mark Yegge

You see that's my point: **choice**. Becoming a millionaire is not about a number. It's about choice. It's about *freedom*, at least for me. I want to have the ability to do whatever I want, within reason, whenever I want to do it and wherever I want to do it. For me that's the ultimate choice.

Maybe for you it's different. Maybe you want to stay home, raise a family and spend your time donating to charity. Whatever it is, I want it to be your choice: your epic choice.

The problem is we only have one life to live, and then it's over. So while we have our chance why don't we make it the most epic life possible? And in order to truly have an epic life you have to have choices and freedom – however you define it. Choices and freedom are made easier, at least in our society, with money.

THE WEALTH CODES

Most of this course is focused on left-brain stuff: formulas, numbers, strategies, etc. But I am a fairly spiritual person and I believe that there is way more to abundance than blindly following a formula. Sure, it helps, but there also needs to be total alignment in your life towards abundance. Your goals, mission, vision, environment, daily rituals, and other things all need to be in harmony with your goals.

Further, there are things that, as humans, we just can't explain when it comes to wealth. Things like synchronicity, serendipity, kismet, and flow, are all manifestations of these unexplained things. Have you ever been thinking about someone, and then your phone rings, and it's them? Have you ever had a goal, wrote it down, and some time later – it happened? I have. These kinds of things happen to me all the time. I can't really explain it. I just believe that there is a universal force, a god, a higher being that helps to make things happen in our lives. And I think that we are all connected somehow. And that connection can be tapped into as assistance.

The Universe has what I call Abundance Codes. Codes that we can each tap into to get what we want. And these codes can be hacked in order to accelerate our path towards abundance. The key elements are covered in depth in this book: 1) vision 2) values 3) financial strategies 4) formulae 5) systems 6) ecology. What we do not cover in depth, but are still an essential part are some of the concepts and practices that help you set up the framework to tap these abundance codes: meditation, mindfulness, prayer, intentions, creative visualization, goal-setting, etc. We have other resources for you to tap into or you can find them on your own, but they are important. So this book is about harnessing the power of the universal force, the universe, source, god, in order to create an abundant life – a life where anything is possible and the pie is infinite.

WHAT THIS COURSE IS ABOUT

This book, course, or manual is part education, part motivation, and part blueprint. We will give you a few strategies, we will ask you questions and ask for you to answer those questions right here in the workbook, and we will help you put a personalized investment blueprint together. What this book is *not* about is teaching you everything there is to know about money, finances, the stock market, credit, etc. There are some great experts in these fields if you want to delve deeper and we have some other courses and resources that we can recommend in some of the critical money areas. But we are not, AirBnB rental people. We are not house-flipping people. We are not Amazon drop-shippers. For those fields, we have partnered with the best resources to teach you the best ways to succeed in those businesses. The same is true for other sectors.

So let's shoot for a nice round number shall we? Let's shoot for $1-million. Once we get to $1-million it's a lot easier to get to the next million. Let's do this together. Let's build a plan together to make you an Epic Millionaire. Ready?

Let's get started.

CHAPTER 2: THE "WHY"

> If you have a big
> enough WHY,
> you can overcome
> any HOW.
>
> *Tony Robbins*

THE WHY

So, the first thing to do is to decide *why* you want to become an epic millionaire. Is it a dream? Is it peer pressure? Is it for an innate desire to make your parents proud? This is a decision that only you can make possibly with some input from some significant people in your life. But at the end it's really your decision. Oh sure, you're going to need some help along the way. You're going to need lots of support and lots of encouragement. You're going to need a team of people to be your cheerleaders. So if you have negative ninnies telling you why you can't do something, then you're going to need to make a change.

You're going to either need to tell them to get on board with your plan and only give you support and encouragement, or you need to have them get off the train because they will only hold you back. We'll talk about this later in the section on ecology and environment and why it is so important, but for now know that this is going to be tough, so you need all of the positive energy you can muster around you. You are going to be making some tough choices and your brain, in addition to many of those around you, is going to want to keep you the same, because that is "safe." No change is safe in neurological terms.

So, back to our WHY. If you have a big enough why, the HOWs will come easily. Let's now focus on why you want to become an epic millionaire. This is important.

In fact, I think this is so important that I'm leaving a spot in this manual for you to fill it in. If you are listening to this book on audio or using an e-book and don't have a spot to write this down, then a journal will do. But please keep it somewhere where you can refer to it often because this will be the cornerstone of your epic millionaire plan.

So I'll ask you again: why do you want to become an epic millionaire?

_____

_____

_____

_____

What will your lifestyle be like?

_____

_____

_____

_____

Write down answers to these questions and as many reasons as you can in the space below:

_____

_____

_____

_____

CHAPTER 3: THE VISION

The most pathetic person in the world is someone who has sight but no vision.

Helen Keller

THE VISION

A vision is a mental picture of the desired result you want - a picture so vivid and emotionally charged that it will help make that result a reality. It's not hope. Hope is not a strategy. It is not a wish. It's a picture of what happens when you get the results you desire, that you work for. A vision in inspired by the future but is brought into the present.

Professional sports teams use vision exercises to improve performance (there is a famous study illustrating that basketball players who practice free throws only by "imagining" the ball going through the basket improve their shooting percentage nearly as much as those who actually throw the ball). I knew someone from a leading college swim team who would visualize his swim, his practice and the real race every day – with emotion. The whole team did this and they became one of the top teams in every swim meet.

Here's why a vision is so powerful:
- A vision inspires action. A powerful vision pulls in ideas, people and other resources. It creates the energy and will to make change happen. It inspires individuals and organizations to commit, to persist and to give their best.
- A vision is a practical guide for creating plans, setting goals and objectives, making decisions, and coordinating and evaluating the work on any project, large or small.
- A vision helps keep organizations and groups focused and together, especially with complex projects and in stressful times.

Not every picture is a vision. Your vision and you should have these traits:

- Be clear
- Be positive
- Be big
- Adjust your attitude
- Adjust your expectations
- Don't overthink
- Come from the heart

What is your vision? (Monthly Income, net worth, lifestyle, people, etc. – describe in detail):

_____

_____

_____

_____

_____

_____

_____

_____

_____

_____

_____

_____

_____

CHAPTER 4: FINANCIAL FREEDOM

_**Financial Freedom:**
When your passive
income exceeds your
expenses._

Great. So you've just determined your *why* and your *vision*. That's a big step! Now let's further define some of the things that we're going to be talking about in this book. The main one is *financial freedom*. Many books talk about it but let's actually define it here.

Financial freedom is when your passive income exceeds your (standard of) living expenses.

That means that if you spend a lot of money, you'll need to make a lot of income. And throughout this course, we are going to be striving to set up your life for **Passive Income**. By the way, passive income is further defined as income that you make without having to *work* for it. We'll talk about that later in the course. For now, just think about passive income as money coming in while you sleep: like from rental payments, book royalties, or interest income. On the other side of the equation, if you can keep your expenses low then it will be easier for you to get to financial freedom.

The problem in our society is that we are victims of it. What? In the United States 70% of our economy is driven by consumerism. Consumerism is the need to buy things to satisfy the norms of society. It's the programming that our society gives us so that we can fit in. We always need to have the nicest cars or live in nice homes, or have the latest technology or the biggest TV. We need to dress in nice clothes, and be seen in the nicest places, with the right people. We are bombarded daily with messages from the environment: television, magazines, our schools, our friends, and our family. All believing that, if we have these things, then our lives will be great.

That's the irony of this book. We are talking about becoming an epic millionaire which means we are talking about the goal of money, but let me just clarify that to me life is not about the things I have, but the *experiences* that I have. For me, it's about more stamps on my passport - and more magic moments with the people that I love - than the items that I have.

Take it from me. I've had all of the stuff. I've had waterfront in Florida. I've had the fastest German convertible sports cars. I've owned the fastest airplanes. And you know what? None of it made me happy. I know it's a cliché to say, but it's true. None of that stuff made me happy. So I sold it all, and now my money is spent on experiences around the world. But that's just me. Maybe it's different for you.

But if you want to have financial freedom you'll have to decide at some point where you will stop spending money on your standard of living. The reason that most people don't become millionaires is because they end up spending more and more as they make more and more. Consequently, they never can get ahead, and they always have to keep working. They never amass enough savings to transform it into passive income. Epic millionaires know that if they can live a comfortable life and maintain a certain level of spending without increasing it. Then, as they increase their income, they move towards financial freedom. We'll talk more in detail about how the money flows later in this course. And we will actually show you how to create a blueprint to build your own passive income streams as you move towards financial freedom.

CHAPTER 5: WHAT IS MONEY?

Too many people spend money they earned, to buy things they don't want, to impress people they don't like.

Will Rogers

WHAT IS MONEY?

This course is all about getting you to a goal. But in order to get you to a goal you must start with the mindset. So let's agree on some definitions. Let's figure out this question: what is money?

Stored Labor. Stored Energy. Freedom. There are many definitions, but money is essentially *stored labor*. You provide value (work, for example), you get paid. That money is now able to be spent in other places so you've stored your labor and now you can exchange that labor for goods and services.

Money is *energy*. It's true. It really is. It can be seen as stored energy and there's a certain something about money that is energetic. Don't you know those people that no matter what they do, everything turns to gold? And there are other people that everything they touch turns into crap? That is because money is attracted to where it's needed and wanted the most. Money flows to where it's appreciated. And money being seen as positive energy, manifests as such so, if you have positive energy around money, you will attract more of it. Plus, you will attract it in an almost-effortless manner.

However, if you have negative energy around money, you will push money away. I've seen it happen over and over again. It's funny, after you lived a certain number of years, you start to see patterns. If I meet someone new, I can very quickly see their *money patterns*. Some people call it their money blueprint. And it all starts from beliefs around money.

Beliefs. Like all beliefs, we aren't born with them. Instead, we learn them from our environment - usually our parents, friends, social media, etc. If you are raised to think that rich people are bad, chances are you probably don't have a lot of money. Even if you get it, the energy of the money will flow away from you because you don't *want* to be rich, at least in your unconscious mind. It's because being rich equals being bad in your own mind.

Think about the programming you had in your environment. Did you ever hear that money doesn't grow on trees? Did you ever hear that the poor and meek will inherit the earth? Did someone around you tell you that it is easier for a camel to fit through the eye of a needle than for a rich person to get into heaven?

Do you listen to the media these days? Do you listen to the reporting that demonizes the wealthy? Do you believe that rich people need to pay their "fair share?" Are you a believer that if someone has something that you don't have, it's because they were lucky? Do you believe that if someone is rich that maybe that you are entitled to some of it? These and others are *disempowering* beliefs that will rob you of your ability to create a path to financial freedom. If you have any of these beliefs, you must change them immediately. Because if you don't, you won't clear away the neural pathways in your brain that get you to financial abundance.

Empowering beliefs: there are two general kinds of beliefs: empowering beliefs and disempowering beliefs. Empowering beliefs are positive beliefs that clear the way for you to achieve what you want. For example, if you want to learn how to play golf but don't believe you are coordinated enough to play, that might cause you to not ever want to go to the golf course and even try. But if you believe golf can be fun, then that will make your brain want to try to get to the golf course and maybe even take a lesson or two. <u>It's usually one small shift to turn a disempowering belief into an empowering one.</u>

For example, you might have a disempowering belief like "most rich people got money handed to them." Now that's pretty disempowering right (statistics show that it is simply not true)? You can easily transform that belief into an empowering one. Here's an example: "rich people are deserving of the money that they have and that's why they keep it." See the difference? One feels negative and the other feels positive. The challenge for you is to turn all of your negative beliefs into positive beliefs; to turn the disempowering into the empowering.

- Do you have the belief that you should work for everything that you earn?
- Do you believe in working smart rather than working hard?
- Do you believe that rich people exploit poor people and keep them down?
- Do you believe that rich people empower others to have employment because they create jobs in companies for others?
- Do you believe the taxes should be higher on rich people or lower on rich people?
- Do you believe that taxes should be lower on poor people or higher?

Take five minutes in the space below and determine what your money beliefs are? What do you really believe about money? These answers will help you shape the beliefs that you're going to have going forward. If you have some disempowering beliefs, you may have to change them in order to open up the opportunities that you want and desire. If you never clear out some of the negative programming, you will never unleash the energy that allows money to be attracted to you. So really, take five minutes or more and take an inventory of your money beliefs. Answer the following questions:

What is money?

_____

_____

_____

_____

What is money, really?

_____

_____

_____

_____

Is there an infinite amount of money or is it limited?

_____

_____

Does it take money to make money?

_____

_____

What will money do for you?

_____

_____

_____

_____

Will money bring you more love? How?

_____

_____

_____

_____

Will money bring you more freedom? How?

_____

_____

_____

_____

Do you need money to be happy? Why?

_____

_____

_____

_____

Now, are there disempowering beliefs that you need to change? Which ones?

_____

_____

_____

_____

Re-write those beliefs into empowering beliefs in the space below:

_____

_____

_____

_____

Now, come up with 5 empowering beliefs around money:

_____

_____

CHAPTER 6: INCOME

Wealth consists, not in having great possessions, but in having few wants.

Epictetus

THE NATURE OF INCOME

Now it's time to talk about how most people earn a living. Most of us exchange our time for money. We work an hour and get paid for an hour's work. The government takes its cut, we take the rest, and we spend it. Then we have to go work another hour to replace what we just spent.

I'm not knocking this, because is how it is how most of us need to start out. This is normally called a job (J.O.B) and for some people it stands for "just over broke." As cute as that sounds, it's actually more true than it sounds. The philosophy that I'm talking about towards becoming an epic millionaire in this book is to *move away from **time equaling money*** as soon as possible.

One hour of time normally equals one hour of pay or one unit of pay. The goal is to move first to the next level where our one hour of time spent, yields multiple units of pay. Eventually we will get to the level where no time spent will get you multiple units of pay (passive income).

ACTIVE INCOME VS. PASSIVE INCOME

Exchanging time for money is *active* income. You work; you get paid. That's what most people think life is about. You work and get paid. Then get up and do it all over again until you die. How depressing.

No. What we want is to create active income for a while. That's cool. But then to get to the point where you **work once** and get paid, paid, paid, paid…..without having to work for that stream of income again. This is called passive income because rather than being an active participant in creating income, you can just sit back and be passive and the income will come in.

Let's not be jaded. You still have to work. But you do it with the intention that you will eventually make income from that work without the actual work continuing.

Here are some examples of how wealthy people use passive income to become financially free:

- Purchase a 100-unit apartment complex and receive rent from 100 tenants each month.
- Invest in a successful restaurant and earn money from a share of the profits
- Loan money for first mortgages to people buying a home and receive interest payments from the borrower
- Set up a short-term (AirBnB) business and receive rental payments
- Set up an Amazon store and sell your items
- Write music and sell on iTunes
- Own a parking garage in a downtown area and earn income from renting your parking spaces.

The list is really endless but most people just think that the only way that they can make money is from working in a job. We will continue to discuss this concept but for now, understand that this entire course is geared towards creating passive income so that you don't *have* to work for your money anymore.

FINANCIAL FREEDOM

When PASSIVE INCOME
Exceeds
Living Expenses

CHAPTER 7: SPENDING

Wealth consists, not
in having great
possessions, but in
having few wants.

Epictetus

SPENDING

(EXPENSES & YOUR STANDARD OF LIVING)

Spending is a subject that is often difficult to discuss because everyone is different. My philosophy is that our society has been programming us since birth to be *consumers*. In fact, seventy percent of our economy is based on spending, or consumerism. From the moment we are born we are bombarded with messages telling us that we need to buy things. We have holidays especially geared to buying our children gifts, and conversely, to make children want gifts. We have holidays that are geared for buying flowers, cards, chocolate, and other items. We watch television or browse the internet and are told that if we drink the right beer or drive the right car or take the right drug - we will be happy. Obviously, that is seldom the case. Come on! Most marketing messages are simply set up for one thing: the goal of separating us from our money and transferring it into another's bank account. Consider:

> I love money. I love everything about it. I bought some pretty good stuff. Got me a $300 pair of socks. Got a fur sink. An electric dog polisher. A gasoline powered turtleneck sweater. And, of course, I bought some dumb stuff, too
>
> Steve Martin

- Do you really need a Gucci purse or can you survive with a $15 purse from Target?
- Must you have a Mercedes or a BMW or can you get by with a car that costs one tenth the price?

32

- Do you have to wear a $2,000 Armani suit or own $900 Leboutin shoes or can you dress nicely with clothing that costs much less?

Lifestyle

So what is the lifestyle that you want? Have you ever thought about it? Is it based on somebody else's expectations of you? Is it based on your own choices? You see, for most of us our lifestyle is based on our parents' lifestyle (or maybe the opposite of our parents in some cases). And by and large, the way our parents live their lives is overall the way we are going to be programmed to live our lives.

Have you ever sat down to think of what you really want out of life? Have you ever thought about how you want to live a day-to-day existence? Well let's do that now! Take a few moments to be intentional about the following questions and their answers. After all it is your life:

How do you want to choose to live your life?

_____

_____

_____

_____

Who will be by your side on a regular basis?

_____

_____

_____

_____

How will you spend your time?

_____

_____

_____

_____

What is the reason that you get out of bed every morning?

_____

_____

_____

_____

_____

_____

Let's talk about your ideal day. What do you do after you wake up?

_____

_____

_____

_____

_____

_____

What hobbies do you participate in on a regular basis?

_____

_____

_____

_____

_____

_____

Are there business pursuits that occupy your time?

_____

_____

In what ways do you give back on a regular basis?

_____

_____

_____

_____

Maybe you're not *there* yet. So what are the realistic expectations of how you want to live your life? Maybe now is a good time to talk about *deferred gratification*. **Deferred gratification** is a concept that says: I will give up something now in order to gain a multiple reward in the future.

So, while you might be able to go out and lease a brand new BMW and bind yourself to the insurance and monthly payments of that choice, it may not be your wisest choice. Let's assume you are spending $1,000 per month on the payment, insurance, etc. on that choice. Could that $12,000 a year be spent better on something else so that in the future you can have a multiple reward? That multiple reward could be a piece of income property that earns you $1,000 per month. Interesting!

To sum it up, consider that you could get a used car that only costs you $5,000 in cash – one time, and then invest to earn money in the future? You still get from point A to point B, maybe in less style, but in the future, you could actually have MORE style because you will be able to buy the BMW itself for cash, if you choose.

So now let me ask the following questions:

What do you really need in order to survive?

_____

_____

_____

_____

In what kind of dwelling? Where can you live?

_____

_____

_____

_____

What kind of transportation do you need?

_____

_____

_____

_____

Instead of dining out, are you able to cook and save between 30 and 50 percent on every meal?

_____

_____

_____

_____

Can you buy just a few key items of clothing and wear them many times instead of purchasing new clothing every season?

_____

_____

_____

_____

Can you travel? If so, how can you make it "affordable?"

_____

_____

_____

_____

Need vs. Want

For the above questions, you have to decide what you really need vs. what you really want. Sure, we all want to drive the BMW or the Ferrari, live in the nice home, wear the latest fashions, fly first class, but do we really NEED it? You make the choice of what you want vs what you need understanding that, for each "upgraded" choice now, you may be giving up an even nicer choice in the future, because you are giving up the power of compounding on the value of that item today.

CHAPTER 8: YOUR BUDGET

A budget tells us what we can't afford, but it doesn't keep us from buying it.

William Feather

YOUR BUDGET

Let's make this quick and painless. I know. I know. You've heard this a million times: you have to set a budget and live within it. It sounds so easy, so why is it so hard? Well, it's not really. It is just a little uncomfortable because it shines a light on your habits and may cause you to feel ashamed. (Remember, your brain wants to keep you safe.)

Well, whatever your feelings, let's get over it and just view a budget as a tool. It's really just a map of your spending that tells you where you are so that you can get control. You want more control, don't you? OK.

Let's just do a simple budget. Below is a sample sheet that you can fill out to do your budget. If you are good with spreadsheets, you can use one to do a budget and if you REALLY want to do it, you can use one of the free online tools like mint.com or even a bank or brokerage firm.

Let's just start here. Simply fill out your most recent numbers of your income and expenses. The key here is to write EVERYTHING down so that you have a true picture of your income and spending.

Monthly Budget

Frugal Fanatic

Items	Budget Amount	Actual Amount	Difference	Notes
INCOME				
Income Total				
Other Income				
EXPENSES				
Mortgage/Rent				
Household Maintenance				
Taxes				
Insurance				
Electricity				
Water				
Sewage				
Gas				
Phone				
Trash				
Cable				
Cell Phone				
Groceries				
Entertainment				
Charity/Donations				
Fuel				
Auto Insurance				
Car Payment				
Child Care				
Credit Cards/Debt				
Loans				
Child Support				
Clothing				
SAVINGS				
Retirement				
College				
Basic/Other				
TOTALS				

Total Income - Total Expenses $ _____

43

Once you have completed your budget, know that it will change. That is its nature. You should also now be armed and able to make decisions with your newly-found budget knowledge.

CHAPTER 9: MINDSET AND ECOLOGY

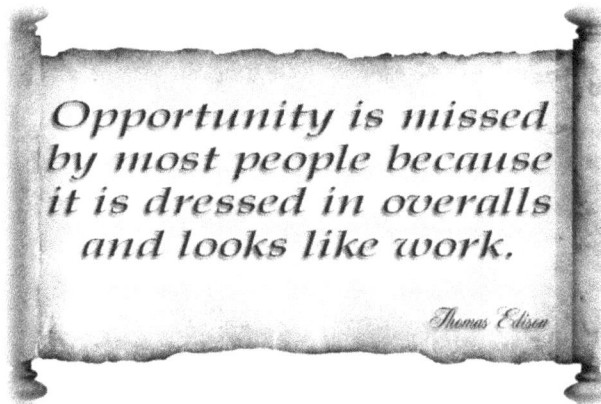

Opportunity is missed
by most people because
it is dressed in overalls
and looks like work.

Thomas Edison

MINDSET AND ECOLOGY

To be wealthy, you have to have a wealthy mindset. Without it, you are doomed to a life with scarce resources. With a wealthy mindset, you remove barriers to wealth and actually create a channel whereby money can flow to you.

You must clear out the negative programming when it comes to money and your mindset. One easy way to do this is too choose an idol or hero that has the financial resources that you would like to have in your life. It can be someone famous or maybe not so famous. The idea is to choose someone that has the characteristics of someone that you would like to emulate. This is a shortcut technique called **modeling** whereby you will "model" someone who has already done what you desire. In theory, you will avoid making the mistakes that have already been made and can simply model best-practices to get your desired outcome.

You see, money makes you more of who you already are. So if you're an asshole, you just become an asshole with a lot of money. If you're likable, you just become more likable. So choose someone who has the traits that you admire.

Money makes you more of who you already are.

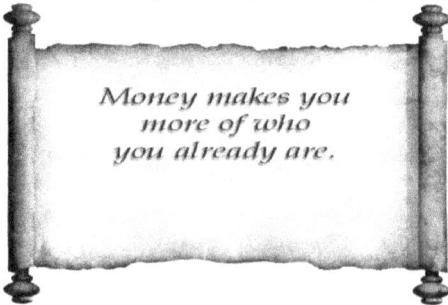

Which Money Role-Model do you choose?

_____

_____

_____

Now list those traits below:

_____

_____

_____

_____

Now whenever you come across a negative wealth belief, your challenge is to ask yourself if your role-model, hero, or idol would have that same belief or a different one. Concurrent with a great money mindset, you should attempt to surround yourself with like-minded people or people on a similar path as you.

After we are born, we look around us to emulate those who care for us. When our parent smiles; we smile. When a parent frowns; we frown. We learn voice inflection from our parents. Scientists have discovered that the reason for this is because of 'mirror neurons' which cause our brains to emulate the people around us. So, if we are going to surround ourselves with losers, chances are we have a better chance of becoming a loser than a winner. If we choose to surround ourselves with people who are wealthy, or at least are dedicated to the path of becoming wealthy, then we have a better chance of building wealth ourselves.

Your tribe attracts your vibe and vice versa; your vibe attracts your tribe. Choose those around you wisely. Many people will try to hold you back from pursuing your dreams. Don't let them. Be careful who you take your advice from. Start to eliminate negative people and those who hold you back from pursuing your dreams in your life. This may often be difficult because some of the closest people around you are your family. So here is an empowering belief for this difficult situation and it's Tony Robbins who says it well: **love your family, choose your tribe**.

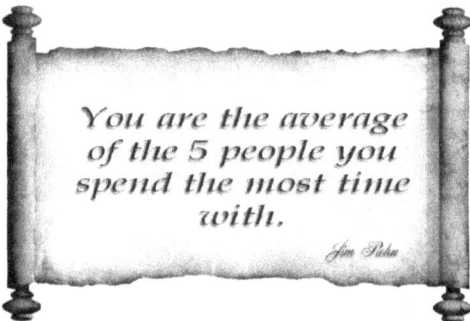

> *You are the average of the 5 people you spend the most time with.*
>
> Jim Rohn

Also it may help to understand that when people try to hold you back, they are doing it for reasons that are not necessarily bad. They just don't want to lose you and they are afraid if you succeed, you will leave them behind and they *will* lose you. The day might come when you must be very frank with them. Let them know that you are on a journey and that you need supportive people around you. If they will be supportive, then you will bring them on the journey with you; but if they will not be supportive and criticize you and are negative, then let them know that there may be times where you will have to be on that journey without them.

Ecology

On incredibly important component of being an Epic Millionaire is to have an epic environment, an eco-system that supports your success. It is essentially what you would expect:

- A positive mindset
- Supportive people around you
- Great mentors
- Few distractions
- Effective Tools

These elements serve to make up your ecology, your environment. Take this seriously because it is easy to be influenced by your environment. As an example, do you think that it is easy to be a financial success when one is born in an environment with a broken home, gang violence all around them and their best mentors are thugs? Do you think they have a good chance of success if that is their ecology? It is possible, but certainly harder.

Be intentional about what is in your ecology and you will have a much better chance of succeeding.

Thermostat

Everyone has a financial or money "thermostat" whether they like it or not. That is, a regulator that governs their mental capacity to generate and accumulate wealth. Like a regular thermostat set to 70 degrees: if the temperature goes up, the thermostat will bring it back down to 70 and if the temperature goes down the thermostat will raise it up to 70 – automatically. The cliché holds true that eight out of ten people who win the lottery lose it all within five to ten years and are often worse off than before they won the lottery. That is because their financial thermostat cannot handle the increased wealth that they encounter. They are still operating with the same money mindset, financial blueprint, and financial thermostat that they had before they won the lottery.

CHAPTER 10: THE MAP TO FINANCIAL FREEDOM

THE MAP TO FINANCIAL FREEDOM

The path to financial freedom is like the path to doing something great? First, you have to start with the fundamentals; then build on them. If you want to be a great skier - at a championship level - you can't just go to the top of a double black diamond and become a great skier at a championship level. You have to take it one step at a time - from the very beginning.

And building a path to financial freedom is like baking a cake. You don't just turn the oven on and pull the cake out and there it is. What you must do is use the recipe ingredients in the order that they were given. And if you do everything right, at the end, out comes a cake.

But let's back up just a bit. Let's set a conscious intention to embark on this path to financial freedom, not just to be wealthy, but rather for what that wealth can do for others. If you approach wealth from this point-of-view, you will have an easier time generating it. If you approach it all from a selfish point of view ("I wanna be really rich"), then it will probably make your journey along the path much harder. Money goes where it is welcome. Money is energy. And money flows to where it can do the most good. So get aligned with a greater purpose than yourself and then begin to map out your road map.

The path to financial freedom entails several levels. Each level sets up the next level. Each level builds on the prior level. And once one level is achieved you never stop.

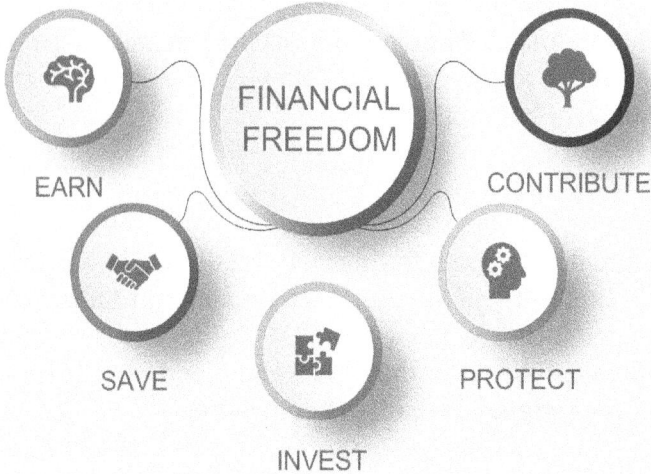

The levels or steps which you must master are:
1. Learn to **Earn**
2. Earn to **Save**
3. Save to **Invest**
4. Invest to **Replace***
5. Replace to **Protect**
6. Protect to **Contribute**

LEARN TO EARN

The first level is learn to earn. Like any skill that we want to master we have to first learn the fundamental steps to it. Our society does a fairly decent job at teaching us things, at least the things that society has deemed worth learning. In this area it programs us to go to school at a very young age when were most apt to be learning. And it starts out with some very small and easy things to accomplish: reading, writing, math, basic rudimentary communications skills like playing with other children. Once we learn to read then they introduce history, language, biology, anatomy and others. Each of these subjects attempts to build on prior knowledge. The English becomes more complex. The sciences become more detailed. So, yes if you want to do anything great you have to first learn the skill; you have to invest the time.

In order to become expert in anything, you must go through the four levels to mastery.

- Unconscious incompetence. That's when you aren't even aware of what you don't know.
- Conscious incompetence. Now you know what you don't know and how hard you must work to get through that level.
- Conscious competence. You now know that you can do something and you can do it at a decent level; you're proficient. You're not an expert yet and you know it and you know it will take even more skills and practice and coaching.

- Unconscious competence. This is the "expert" level where you don't even have to think about what you know, and how much you know. It just happens naturally and it is almost as if you were born with the skill.

To illustrate the 4 levels, let's use the basic example of driving. When you first drive, you're not fully aware of the different components of driving: the steering wheel, the accelerator, the brakes, even the clutch and the gears. Then there's the *feel* of all of those things. Once you become aware of them, you realize how much you don't know about how to use them all let alone using them all at the same time. This is **unconscious incompetence**: you don't know what you don't know. There is much to learn.

Once you have started to familiarize yourself with each of the components of driving as you start to put it into practice, you still have to learn how to use them all

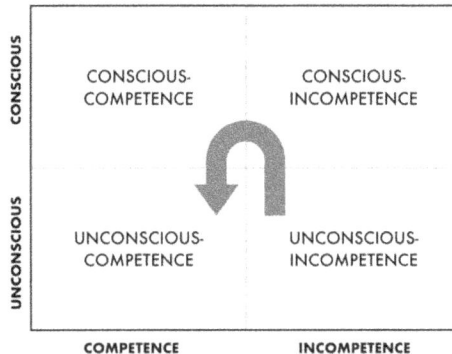

	COMPETENCE	INCOMPETENCE
CONSCIOUS	CONSCIOUS-COMPETENCE	CONSCIOUS-INCOMPETENCE
UNCONSCIOUS	UNCONSCIOUS-COMPETENCE	UNCONSCIOUS-INCOMPETENCE

together. You realize how many mistakes you make: maybe you are corrected by your driving coach or your parent. Often, you may even know the mistakes that you're making and you can't stop making the mistake! This is **conscious incompetence**: you know what you don't know.

Once you have driven for a few hours, have a feel behind the wheel, and have been through some interesting situations in traffic, you now begin to feel as if you understand the skill of driving. You know that if someone cuts you off, you can just brake or swerve (even make a gesture) as you continue to drive. You can do all of these things without really thinking about them too much. This is the level of **conscious competence**: you know what you know.

At this point, the more hours that you invest in the skill, the better you become at it. In fact, you can start adding in other non-essential skills at the same time you were doing all of those other driving skills that were so hard to master at first. It's easy for you now to turn on the radio, to change the station on the radio, to answer a phone call and talk on the phone as you continue to drive. In fact there will be times where you arrive at your destination without even knowing how you actually got there. All of the driving skills took place at an unconscious level. You didn't have to even think about it consciously. Your brain did it for you. That allows your conscious brain to be able to focus on new skills and other things that you could master or take on as you continue to unconsciously use the skills of driving. This is the mastery level, the expert level, known as **unconscious competence**: you don't have to think about what you know. Malcolm Gladwell, in his book Outliers, describes how a level of roughly ten thousand hours devoted to a skill is required to put you at a level of mastery.

So where are we going with all of this? The answer is that we are emphasizing that the importance of learning (learning to learn) is a skill that we must master early. We are going to need to learn how to *map* our way to financial freedom. In our first level of financial freedom, learn to earn, we must *learn* a skill that will allow us to **earn** money. To learn any certain skill, our

society encourages attending a higher institution of knowledge like a college or university or sometimes a trade school. For example, if you want to be a lawyer you will need a four-year college degree in the United States and then three years of subsequent law school. Next, in order to ensure that you have mastered the knowledge of law school, you have to sit for a grueling (bar) exam in order to be even given the right to be able to practice what you have learned. You may have to take on some internships to actually learn how the job skills are accomplished at the job site. And once you have passed the bar exam you may take on your first legal job. Wow! What a process! (but you are not done yet)

Often, to be successful, you must endure grueling hard work as a junior attorney, doing the mundane research work for the more senior lawyers. You will also have to learn the job skills of client acquisition and client management. You may do this for years until maybe one day you are recognized by the senior partners and are allowed to buy in to the law practice becoming a Junior Partner. Eventually you may work your way into becoming an Equity or Senior Partner but that may take many more years. So through this progression we see that the first step is **learning to earn**.

The smarter you are about your learning, the more income you can potentially make. So often the young people in our society choose their occupation with little care. Since they make this decision poorly in the beginning, it is often a regret for the rest of their life. Most of our young people are not guided properly in how to select a suitable field of study. By "suitable" I mean a field that is suited to their temperament AND is something that will come easy to them AND will have the potential to earn a lot of money.

57

This issue unfortunately creates a lot of art history and political science majors who graduate and have broad general education (often about impractical things) but have dim prospects for getting a job. But I digress. The point here is that if you're going to learn to earn, make sure that you're learning a skill that translates into the potential for high income in your lifetime. This goes back to your vision so really spend some time working on your vision section to clearly outline the vision for your life.

EARN TO SAVE

In this level on the path to financial freedom, you will be earning money. Now, most of the money that you earn will be used to live on but you must start *saving* now, early and as soon as possible, without going into substantial debt. You are not saving just for savings sake. You are saving because it will be the engine to catapult you to financial freedom. Saving allows you to invest. But investing doesn't just mean saving for retirement. Eventually the path to financial freedom means that you invest so that you can create other income streams which will replace your working income, your earned income.

So as you earn, you will also save. We discuss standard-of-living in a different area of this course. For now, just understand that saving is going to give you the stored-energy and create an engine for investing. **Plan to save ten to twenty percent of every element of income that you make now for the rest of your life**. In the Richest Man in Babylon, a book by George S. Clason, the main character in the book saves ten percent of all of his income

and that makes him the richest man in the society. You see, by saving ten to twenty percent of every element of income that you make, you learn to live on a smaller percentage of your income. You don't miss the amount that's pulled out of your income and that is the real secret to financial freedom.

SAVE TO INVEST

In this level on the path to financial freedom, the money that you've begun to save is now earmarked for investments. A good portion of the rest of this volume will be dedicated to how to invest, and we have other resources available for you as well. I hope that you understand that at this level, the learning never ends. This is where many people often fail. They hand their money off to a financial expert and expect the expert to treat their money with the care and concern that they would themselves treat their money. This often does not happen and people give up their power in their investments. Don't be one of them. You must learn the skills to invest just as you learned the skills to earn because once you start making enough money from your income and investments, you will eventually spend much more of your time managing that.

If you invest correctly, you will begin to amass of fortune that you could not have even considered when you first began this journey. This investment income and growth will eventually replace your earned income and then you can retire and become financially free – or keep working and become financial free. You decide! Hopefully you won't have to do this when you're sixty-five or seventy years old but if you apply the principles in this book you can do it much earlier at thirty, forty, fifty, or even sixty years old. You can then do what you want, wherever you want, with whom you want, anytime that you want....and isn't that the goal? Financial freedom?

INVEST TO REPLACE (PASSIVE INCOME)*

In this stage, you are working on your investments with the goal that your investment income will eventually replace your working income. Hey, isn't that what

INCOME

ACTIVE	PASSIVE
Derived from the active practice of a profession or business	Derived from income generating assets/investments

your retirement plan and Social Security are supposed to do anyway? Well, why not accelerate the timeline so that you don't have to wait until 62, 65 or 70 years old to start reaping the rewards of all of your sacrifice? Let's bring that view into the near future.

Once you open yourself to this possibility, you will begin to align towards it. But it is a vision shift because our society wants you to "work hard" until you are no longer

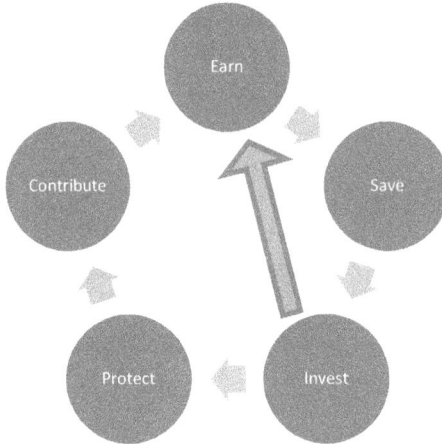

needed and then you can retire. But what is retirement? I know that, for most people, they work hard all of their lives and then once they get to retirement age, they are just, well.....tired. So they sit around and watch TV and basically wait until they die. This is one way to look at retirement and it is unfortunately, all too common. This is voluntary suicide!

But why does this happen? What happened to all of the dreams and the hopes for retirement? Here are, what I believe, the main reasons that retirement will always stay just a dream for some:

- You are just tired from working for forty-plus years and just want to take a break
- You don't have as much money as you thought you would have to pursue your dreams
- Your health has declined so you don't feel that you can travel, or pursue some of those adventures that you would have pursued if you were younger

- You are afraid of being away from your family
- You are afraid of being away from your doctors
- You just don't have the energy to go places anymore
- You don't have people to do things with because they have died or moved away or are still working
- You are afraid of running out of money
- You have sacrificed for your kids' education or their wedding and didn't plan well for yourself
- …. And many others….

However, if you start a plan NOW to invest in your abundant financial future, you won't be one of these people just trying to get to retirement age so that you "can then enjoy life." You will be someone who can enjoy financial freedom much earlier; and you will have time to give back to others – and enjoy the process!

Wouldn't it be great if you could get out of the daily work grind, but still have money coming in? Remember, money is stored energy and your goal is to transfer that energy into passive income – money that comes in while you are NOT working for it. This is the true secret of ultimate wealth and it is what the wealthy people in our society have been doing for hundreds of years while others have worked for THEM. Pretty smart, huh?

It's your turn to be smart by learning the path to financial freedom through passive income.

REPLACE TO PROTECT

Once you start to amass your fortune, others will want it. Think about people who win the lottery. Family and friends start to come at them asking for their money because "they can afford it." Often, they are faced with either loaning (giving) them money or face losing them in their life. They don't want to lose those important people in their life, so they give away their fortune, often losing control of their money in the process.

Alternatively, people see people who have assets as wealthy and they can often feel entitled to some of that wealth. There are just some bad apples in our society who think that they should just be able to sue wealthy people and get their assets for themselves. Now, maybe some of these suits are legitimate, but often they are not. Either way, as someone who has worked hard, earned, saved and invested, you want to be smart and protect yourself from financial ruin. This course itself is not about protection as we cover that more in depth in other areas of our teachings, but you should know that once you begin this journey to financial freedom, you should protect yourself.

Here are a couple of ways that wealthy people, and you eventually, will protect your assets and your life's work:

- Insurance – protect your business, property, and your wealth by spreading the risk through insurance. Normally, you won't need it, but when you do, you won't lose everything you have due to litigation or loss.

- Corporate structure – you must learn how to structure corporations so that nobody will want to go through the trouble of trying to take your assets.
- Debt – using debt can be a way to keep your creditors at bay. Proper debt structure techniques are important to learn.
- Diversification – not keeping all of your eggs in one basket makes it more difficult to get at your assets.
- Partnerships – having the right partners can help you minimize your risks

The bottom line: as you grow your assets, learn the techniques required to protect them and yourself from loss.

PROTECT TO CONTRIBUTE

For many, this is what life is about: helping others less fortunate. You will become more fortunate by following the teachings in this course and once you do, you will likely want to help others. You may help them with your resources or your time. You may want to give back by teaching others how to do what you have done. You may want to empower your children or others. You may just want to donate to a worthy cause or volunteer your time. Whatever you do, you will be helping to make the world a better place – and you'll probably feel better about yourself by doing so in the process.

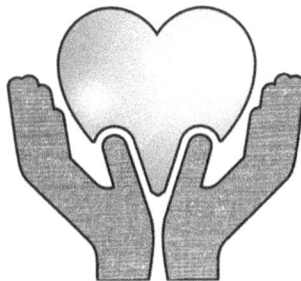

CHAPTER 11: THE FORMULA

Life Is A
Formula.

Mark Gaye

Earn

THE EARNING PHASE is where most of us start out. In fact, isn't that the goal? Don't we go to school so that we can learn at a higher level so that we can earn more and make a living? But why do we make a *living*? Is it just to make money and eat food or are there other reasons to make a living?

Some people never graduate high school and their earning potential, according to conventional wisdom in society, is limited. So many people choose to go to college when they graduate. Others even continue on to graduate school and post-graduate studies getting a masters degrees or a PhD. Conventional wisdom.

But I think in our society we may have lost its way about why we educate ourselves. The theory is that we should go to college and get a degree. But somewhere along the way, we forgot **why** we're getting the degree in the first place. There really is only one reason: so that we can earn money doing something that were good at and enjoy (hopefully). The problem now comes in that many people are "*educated*" but the education does not convert into a practical, applicable way to earn a living. These days there are millions of people who have *worthless* degrees that may have cost hundreds of thousands of dollars. Yet even in an economy that is growing at two or

three percent per year with record unemployment, they still cannot find work. Why? Because the employment landscape is changing. Many years ago just going to college guaranteed that you would get out and get a good job, no matter the degree that you received. You could get a political science degree and start in an entry level position and work your way into a corporation and have a job for life. But things have changed. Things have changed so much and so quickly now that degrees, for just the sake of a certificate or a diploma, don't translate into earnings.

For example, I have many friends who are in the short-term rental business (Air BnB). They buy houses, fix them up, and rent them out for a few nights at a time. Some of them are now financial millionaires and they are in a business that they enjoy very much. But the last time I checked, I didn't see colleges offering a degree in the short-term rental business. I know dozens of people who are *house flippers*, but I don't see degrees in house flipping. Some of my friends make over a million dollars a year selling things online: courses, items and books. But I don't see college degrees in online marketing.

So would you rather have a degree in political science or psychology that takes four years and costs one-hundred to three-hundred thousand dollars but yet when you graduate may not even guarantee you a job? Or, should you spend time learning one of the new crafts that this fast changing economy provides that can almost instantly start to make you money and may only cost a few hundred dollars to learn it?

Yes, my friends it's time for us to reevaluate our educational system. I quote my father who used to say, "when everyone in the world is a doctor, I want to be the garbage man." What did he mean by that? Well, a few things. Because of supply and demand, not every job is needed. Next, just because a job takes ten years to be trained doesn't mean that it is any better than a job that may take two years or less to learn.

Many of the *trades* (like plumbing, electrical work, carpentry, even online marketing, etc.) now pay six-figure salaries. Other occupations that are not even discussed in colleges now have become fantastic occupations financially because so few people want to do them or are trained in them.

So the point here is this: don't just let society tell you what you should do. Make a choice! Make a choice based on data and realism.

The Earnings Allocation Formula (EAF)

So now I want to introduce you to the core of this book or course. It's called the earnings allocation formula or the EAF. You see, if you do things according to a formula then you can repeat them with the same results. If you bake a

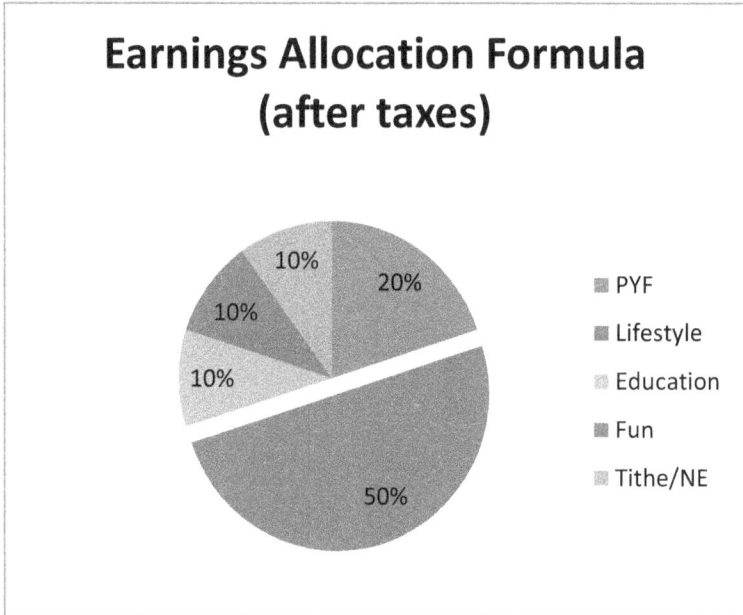

Earnings Allocation Formula (after taxes)

10%
10%
10%
20%
50%

- PYF
- Lifestyle
- Education
- Fun
- Tithe/NE

really great chocolate cake and you follow the recipe then you should be able to repeat that recipe over and again rather than having to recreate it.

So here is the recipe for how to save your earned money:
- 20% to Pay Yourself First (PYF) Account
- 50% to Lifestyle (Spending)
- 10% to Education
- 10% to Fun
- 10% to Tithing/New Experiences

69

After you Pay Yourself First (20% remember?), you will allocate your earnings into 4 other accounts as shown in the allocation graph. You can have your bank do this automatically too just as you do for your main savings (PYF) account. That means that you have 5 accounts:

1. **Pay Yourself First (PYF) Account**
2. **Lifestyle (Spending) Account**
3. **Education Account**
4. **Fun Account**
5. **Tithing/New Experiences Account**

Save – Pay Yourself First (PYF)

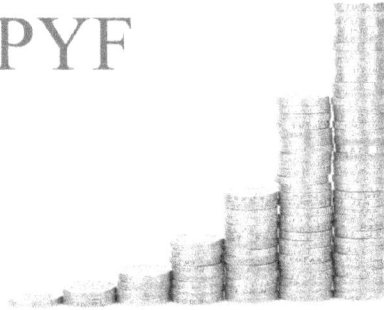

Now let's turn our attention to saving. Saving is another one of those money *programs* or *beliefs* that we were told was important when we were growing up, and it is. But just know that **you'll never save your way to prosperity**. Saving should be for two things: 1) your emergency money and 2) a holding account for funds to be used to invest.

Savings is never an investment in and of itself. Why? Because money generally loses value over time due to inflation. To put it bluntly, the longer money sits idle, the less it can purchase in the future. Money wants to be invested.

In this course, we discuss how much of your earnings you should be saving. Ideally, you should be saving 20% of every dollar that comes to you. It should happen automatically so that you don't have to even think about it.

From there, you have some responsibilities. If you are in debt, then you should start by paying off your debt with half of your savings. That means you earmark 10% (or half of the 20% that you are allocating into savings) until your debt is paid off. The other half, or 10% of your earned dollars, should go into a Sleep Money or Emergency Fund (discussed below). Finally, once your Sleep Money fund is built up, then you can start to allocate that money into investments.

Sleep Money/Emergency Fund

So what is Sleep Money? Sleep money is the amount of money that you need to have in the bank or saved in order to be able to sleep well at night. Many people call it an emergency fund. The bottom line here is that if you lose your job, you should have between three and six months of living expenses saved up to be able to have time to look for new employment or to live comfortably until something new comes along.

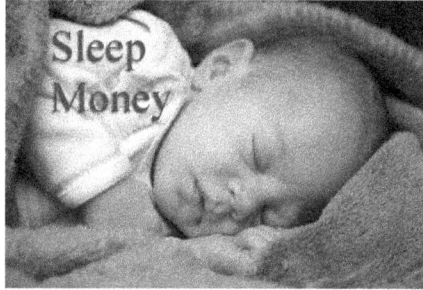

The last thing you want to do is have to take a job that you hate simply because you need to have money to live. That makes for a miserable life and often, once you get into that spiral, you can never get out.

Save 3 to 6 Months Of Living Expenses.

So what are the mechanics of saving according to this philosophy? Well, you need to have your bank help you set up separate accounts. This is critical! This makes saving *automatic* and that gives you about a ninety percent greater chance of succeeding than if it's not automatic. You see, things come up in life. And if the temptation is there to stray from the plan, you probably will. The idea here is to build the habit, and if it's an automatic habit you have a much greater chance for success.

So do it! Set up a separate account that takes 20% of every dollar that goes into your main checking account and transfers it into your savings account. From that savings account take half each month and pay off your debt, and the other half can accrue in savings until it can be invested. You must set this up now. If you want to become a millionaire or multi-millionaire then this is one small habit that can give you a very large reward.

We recommend saving 20% of your after-tax income on in your Pay Yourself First (PYF) account.

Lifestyle: 50%

LIFESTYLE

You must learn to live on fifty percent of your after tax income. That's your spending, your lifestyle or your standard of living account. Your spending includes expenses for dwelling, cable, telephone, transportation, and groceries, with *some* day-to-day entertainment.

You may say, "fifty percent!? F#@&, I can't live on fifty percent!" Well, this is the time to revisit that *want versus need* point. Now, this might shake you up, or it might be just the ticket to propel you to riches. So take an inventory of what you're spending and that means to start with a budget. Write down everything that you're spending money on now, and see what it looks like at the end of a week or even a month (and I mean every item). See if you can find some places to cut your spending.

For example, if you notice that you're spending a hundred dollars on Friday nights for drinks with friends. That's four-hundred dollars per month. Without judging the morals, health and ethics of drinking, ask yourself if you really need it? If you do, then ask yourself if you really need to spend money going out to drink or if you can do it at home for less money. Another example is the amount of money you may spend on dining out. Sure, $10, 20 or even $50 per meal doesn't seem like much, but if you do it twice a day five days a week that's another few hundred dollars per week or even thousands of dollars per month that you're spending on dining out.

Every dollar you spend now is a multiple dollar that you give up later.

You will have to work longer to make it up.

The amount of money that you could save by learning how to cook and eating in and getting the flavor and the satisfaction of home cooking, are benefits that you could gain by learning this one simple craft. Where else could you apply this concept?

So create a simple budget. Discover what you are spending money on and decide what it is that you could cut back on.

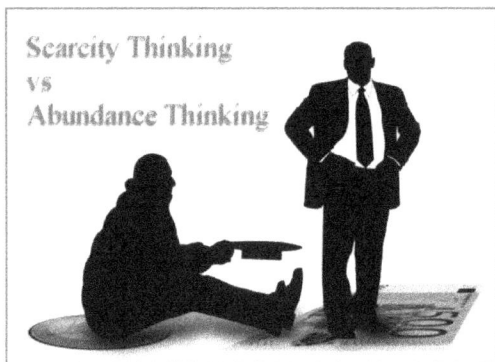

Scarcity Thinking
vs
Abundance Thinking

This, however, is a *scarcity* mindset. It comes from a philosophy of **not having** which is an important part of this whole philosophy.

75

Yet a much more important part of the philosophy is one of an *abundance* mindset. You see with an abundant mindset you live into abundance. You act as if money is an infinite resource - not in a crazy way - in a way that creates a positive flow of money around you.

So you might ask yourself, "how can I make more money to be able to afford my existing lifestyle?" If you are not willing to cut back on expenses (which is ok), then you must increase your earnings (which is even better). The best solution is to do both: cutting back on unnecessary expenses and increasing earnings so that you can live on fifty percent of your after tax earnings. (Oh, there is a third way too, and that is to decrease the amount of taxes you pay (legally, of course).

We recommend spending 50% of your after-tax income on Lifestyle expenses.

Education: 10%

EDUCATION

In a society that is changing at a more exponential rate every month, you must adapt and grow or you will be left behind. Imagine the rocket scientists of the NASA moon landing trying to build a rocket today! Everything has changed. We have more power in our handheld devices than all of the computers required to put a man on the moon. And the technology knowledge base has changed as well. The knowledge today allows us to put up thousands of satellites without a second thought, and at a fraction of the cost of the moon landing of the 1960s. Things are advancing no matter your field, and you better be on top of it lest you be left behind. So, YOU have to take charge of your learning and education in your field or you will be replaced by someone who has.

Unfortunately, even if you have an advanced college degree, you are not guaranteed a job. Further, even if you get a job, you will still have to spend months or years training how that job is done at your organization. And if you want to advance, you must learn leadership and management skills that you may have no training in. So you will always need to spend some of your money on personal development and education. Get used ot it. Embrace it. It's the future and you will be a part of it.

We recommend spending 10% of your after-tax income on Education.

10% Fun

Look. I'm not going to sit here and dictate to you that success with money is all about investing and saving and spending and passive income. At the end of the day, you have to live a life that's worth living. That means you have to have fun. In fact above all else you have to have fun - it's what makes it all worth it. All of the saving and all of the investing and all of the money strategies don't amount to a hill of beans if you don't enjoy the process of life.

So why not make life's *fun* an automatic part of your money strategy? Invest ten percent of your take home earnings into fun. Now this is in your Fun Account. This is a dedicated amount of saving that goes directly to having fun! The requirement here is that you MUST spend it on fun. That means that you have to have a goal for what you are going to spend your fun money on. Let's make it a SMART goal. A SMART goal is one that is specific, measurable, achievable, realistic, and time based. In the space below, describe the goal that you're going to have for your fun money and be sure to to include a date by which you will spend it. Remember, you must spend your fun money. This is not savings. This is for fun. When you save and spend your fun money you must celebrate. This will tell your body and your mind that it's ok to save and to have fun. It will reinforce future Fun goal acheivement.

We recommend spending 10% of your net after-tax income on Fun.

10% Tithing OR 5% Tithing/5% New Experiences (NE)

TITHE or NE

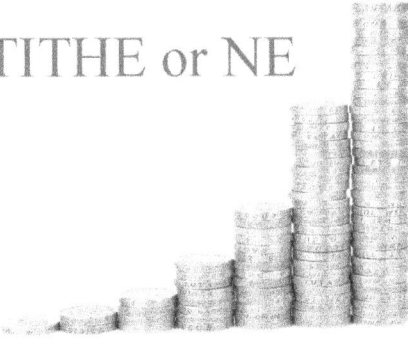

The last ten percent of your take home money will go into a final account. Contribution is an important category and a wonderful habit to build as soon as you can. Many religions ask for regular donations of ten percent of your take home earnings and it is known as *tithing*. If you believe in that concept, then please take ten percent of your take home earnings and donate to your favorite religion, church or charity.

If you would rather split it, that is an option as well. I would recommend that you split it: 5% for tithing or charity, and another five percent for new experiences (NE). I personally love to travel and any of my new experience money goes for travel. But you could spend your five percent on learning how to salsa dance, or to cook, or to learn photography or a musical instrument. Both of these categories are the real juice of life: contributing and experiencing new things.

We recommend earmarking 10% of your net after-tax income for Tithing or 5% for Tithing and 5% for New Experiences.

CHAPTER 12: TAXES

You don't pay taxes.
They take taxes.

Chris Rock

TAXES

I am not a CPA or accountant, thank God! It's just not my thing. So I am not going to talk too much about taxes. It is just something that you need to learn about so that you can keep your accounting people honest and you can plan your financial life without losing control.

The biggest corporations in the country often pay little or no taxes. Don't get mad, they do it legally and you can too. You just need to learn about how they and you can do it.

Now, I know that the section about the Earnings Allocation Formula may have been tough for you. Maybe it was a challenge or wake-up call for you. Or perhaps you are just going to use it as a place to give up because "it's going to be impossible to live on 50% of my take-home pay." How you choose to view the EAF is totally up to you, but if you are a bit uncomfortable, you may want to look at the amount of tax that you pay as a way to find some extra resources.

Taxes are the biggest expense that you will ever pay in your life. Like my Dad's CPA always says, "there are worse things than paying taxes" but honestly I cannot think of many. The government provides a service but there is no way in hell that they spend my money better than I do. I believe that you should pay taxes: **the least amount legally possible**. There is a tax code of thousands of pages and in there are loopholes and deductions that allow you to legally pay little or no taxes.

The tax laws are passed from pressure from lobbyists and special interests with their own agendas. So they leave footprints and those are the same footprints that we can stand in when doing our taxes. Plus, the government tries to give incentives to get the public to do things that will get the government more money, but in a stealthy way.

There are thousands of examples of the above concepts, but I will give you a few here:

1) The government allows tax deductions for charitable giving (because otherwise the government would have to tax you more and then do the charitable activity themselves).
2) The government allows tax deductions for home ownership.
3) The government provides tax deductions for business expenses.
4) The government provides certain deductions or credits for renewable energy.
5) The government provides a tax deduction if you are married or have children.
6) Certain state governments have no personal income tax.
7) The government gives businesses deductions and credits for oil exploration or farming.
8) The government sometimes pays people to NOT farm.

The list is endless. Just get to know the basics for you and eventually your businesses and you will be on the path the keeping more legally that you can use to create even more passive income.

INVESTING CONCEPTS

In the following sections, we will deal with some common investing concepts and some misconceptions around them.

The goal is to get you to think for yourself instead of just espousing the crap that is fed to you by the press, Wall Street, lawyers and others who are sometimes not as interested in helping you, but in making more money for themselves. Often, people who mean well are just not the right people to get advice from. Don't give up your power to them. Again, **think for yourself**.

CHAPTER 13: YOUR HOME

A home is not an asset. It is a luxury.

Mark Yegge

YOUR HOME – AN INVESTMENT?

So many politicians, parents, media and others fill our head with a concept that, in my opinion, is now pure propaganda. The concept: "owning your own home is the American Dream; it is an asset." Bullshit!

I've owned several homes and let me tell you, it's no dream. I'll give you the business reasons in a minute, but let me just tell you how much owning a home can be the opposite of a dream. First, you have to pay for it. Since most people don't have the money to pay cash, they borrow to buy it, which means that they have to pay interest on the borrowed money (big expense). Second, you must pay to maintain the home - a new roof recently cost me $25,000 – (big expense again). And think about all of the other big expenses: bathrooms, kitchens, appliances, landscaping, pools, docks, seawalls, etc. Third, you must pay property taxes on the home (big expense). Finally, you have maintenance expenses for the yard, the pool, and the countless other nit-picky things that must be maintained when you own a home. All of this adds up to big expenses and, if you are going to do the work yourself, lost time.

No my friend, your house is not an asset. In today's world if you want to be a financial success, you have to know the difference between an asset and a liability. One of the
reasons so many people struggle financially today is because they're calling their liabilities 'assets.' Your house is not an asset. Your car is not an asset. If you understand a

financial statement, a skill you should master by the way, listed on the balance sheet are assets and liabilities.

Put simply, an asset puts money in your pocket and a liability takes money from your pocket. So for most people, their houses are not assets but rather liabilities because each month it takes money *from* you to live in the house. Even if you pay cash for the home or don't have a mortgage, you still have insurance, maintenance and capital repairs.

Now, I'm not saying "don't buy a house." Just know that it is not usually your asset. If you bought a house and rented it out for more than cost, it would usually put money into your pocket: Asset. But if it takes money away from you, it is a liability. In business, it all comes down to cash flow. If money flows in, it is an asset and if money flows out, it is a liability. To be really simple, increasing assets moves you *towards* your goal of being a millionaire or multi-millionaire. Increasing liabilities, moves you *away*.

In fact, the bank will list your house (the loan that they gave you) as an asset on their books because it brings them money every month. But you will list your house on your own balance sheet as a liability because you must pay the mortgage every month. It cannot be an asset to both you AND the bank.

So, of course, you must live somewhere, and it will cost something to live somewhere. Just don't be deluded into the thought that the American Dream is to own your own home because now you know how to think about it from a business perspective.

CHAPTER 14: DEBT

> The man who never
> has money enough to
> pay his debts, has too
> much of something
> else.
>
> *James Lendall Basford*

LET'S TALK ABOUT DEBT

Good vs. Bad Debt

One school of thought today is that ALL debt is bad because it makes you a slave to the lender. Is this true? Well, there are two kinds of debt: good debt and bad debt and there IS a difference. Let's explore.

Debt is simply borrowing. When you borrow, you must factor in why you are borrowing, the amount, the cost and the terms of the money. Simply, if someone loaned you money at say, 10%, but you KNEW that you could make 50%, that means that you could make a 40% net return. That's a pretty good reason to borrow money. So that debt is good. If you borrowed money that had an interest rate of 25% to buy something that was losing value quickly, then that is bad debt. See the difference? Debt can be a killer or it can be a tool. Not all debt is equal.

Debt can be used as leverage. It's a tool when used properly and responsibly. It gets you to where you want to go faster.

Let's start by defining *good debt*. Good debt is something that helps increase your wealth over time. This could be the purchase of income-producing property, an asset that is throwing off value periodically like rental income.

Bad debt is essentially the opposite. Bad debt lowers your wealth over time. This would be an item like a car or groceries or other things that decline in value or take money away from you regularly. Most cars lose value from the moment of the first purchase, they depreciate or lose value over time.

Let's test this out with a few examples. For each example, try to think if it is good or bad debt. (Answers are found somewhere else in this course)

If you use debt for the following is it Good Debt or Bad Debt?

1) Buying a bedroom set.
2) Purchasing a television.
3) Getting new tile for your rental apartment
4) Putting Friday night drinks on your credit card.
5) Loaning money to a friend for 3 months, no interest.
6) Loaning money to your Dad to use to buy $50,000 in restaurant equipment for the pizzeria that has been open for 10 years, 7% interest, 2 year payback.
7) Buying a duplex for $100,000 which is already rented and makes $10,000 per year. The $100K that you borrow is at 12%.
8) Found a great deal on your next home: house worth $500K, on the market for 18 months, you can get it for $400K and pay 6% interest.

ANSWERS:

1) Bad debt. Item loses value (depreciates) over time.
2) Bad debt. Item loses value (depreciates) over time.
3) Depends. If it will help you rent it out for more money, then Good debt.
4) Bad debt. Money is gone.
5) Tough one. Money is probably gone, but if not, you should at least charging interest to your friend for the cost of the money. It is a business transaction, not a gift.
6) Good debt. Your money should appreciate over time by 7% as long as the business stays open and you are paid back.
7) Trick question. Bad debt. The income is only 10% but you will be paying 12% on the money so you will lose at least $2,000 on this duplex – all other things equal.
8) Bad debt. First of all, it is a home, so it takes money away from you. Second, just because it seems like a good deal doesn't mean that it is. It was on the market for a year and a half so you may not be able to sell it for what you paid. Be careful.

Summary: use debt properly as a tool to increase your wealth over time and you won't have to worry about debt. Just don't pile up too much of it because markets change and even good debt can sometimes turn against you. But certainly don't let debt be used on declining value items or "assets" that pull money away from you. Know the difference between good and bad debt.

Debt Can Snowball

While this is not meant to be a course on debt or credit cards or borrowing, you should know the ramifications of debt it is not used properly. Most debt is easily amassed on credit cards (Americans now spend 113% of their income) and credit cards are paid for by your payments. Usually they charge above-average interest rates. If you don't pay your balances off regularly, the interest rates and unpaid borrowed amount can start to compound quickly and the debt can grow to such levels, that it becomes difficult or impossible to pay off. Don't let this snowball happen to you. When you are in a hole, the first thing that you must do is "stop digging." Make a goal to stop spending on bad debt. Next, ensure that you are pro-active on paying off as much of your bad debt as quickly as you can so that you can get ahead of it.

Get Out Of Debt

In order to avoid the dreaded snowball just described, you should make a real effort to pay those balances off quickly. There are many ways to do so, but let me suggest just a few to begin:

- Sell off the things that you don't use anymore or even regularly. My sister had a bunch of china and real silverware that she only used once a year. She turned that into several hundred dollars.

- Have a garage or yard sale. Those little items add up. Every time I've held a garage sale, I was amazed that I made $800, $1,500 or even $3,100.

- Pay off your smallest balances first OR

- Pay off your highest-interest balances first.

- Grab a side-job or weekend work to get those balances paid off.

TIP: only spend <u>cash</u> to buy things that decline in value or take money from you over time.

I hope by now you can see that bad debt can wreak havoc on your finances and you must get control of this aspect of your life. Good spending habits combined with an avoidance of bad debt will have a multiplied effect on your chances of financial success.

Cost of Money

Just a quick concept: debt costs money. Like anything in life, there is a cost to anything worthwhile. If money doesn't cost too much (interest rate is relatively low), then you can use it as a tool to increase in values that earn more than the cost of money. So if money is cheap, think of it as a great tool to help you increase your wealth.

CHAPTER 15:
INVESTMENTS

Investment in
knowledge pays the
best interest.

Ben Franklin

INVEST

There are literally thousands of types of investments. This is a quick description of some of the most popular. *(CREDIT: FINRA for the great descriptions)*

Stocks

When you invest in a stock, you become one of the owners of a corporation. Stocks represent ownership shares, also known as equity shares. Whether you make or lose money on a stock depends on the success or failure of the company, which type of stock you own, and what's going on in the stock market overall and other factors.

Stocks and stock mutual funds often can be an important component of a diversified investment portfolio. Learn more about different types of stocks and how to assess whether a given stock is right for you.

Bonds

A bond is a loan an investor makes to a corporation, government, federal agency or other organization in exchange for interest payments over a specified term plus repayment of principal at the bond's maturity date. There are a wide variety of bonds including Treasuries, agency bonds, corporate bonds, municipal bonds and more. Likewise there are many types of bond mutual funds.

When you invest in bonds and bond mutual funds, you face the risk that your investment might lose money, especially if you bought an individual bond and want or need to sell it before it matures. And bond mutual fund prices can fluctuate, just as stock mutual funds do. Risk will also vary depending on the type of bond you own.

Bonds and bond mutual funds often can be an important component of a diversified investment portfolio. Whether you are just starting out or a seasoned investor, we have an array of articles, tools and resources to help learn more about bond investing

Investment Funds

Investment funds pool the money of many investors and invest according to a specific strategy. Funds come in various types, each with differing features. Generally, publicly offered funds—such as mutual funds, exchange-traded funds, closed-end funds and unit investment trusts—must be registered with the Securities and Exchange Commission (SEC) as investment companies. Private investment funds (often called hedge funds) are often exempt from registration.

Funds can offer diversification and professional management—and they can feature a wide variety of investment strategies and styles. As with any security, investing in a fund involves risk, including the possibility that you may lose money. And how a fund performed in the past is not an indication of how it will perform in the future.

Some funds, such as hedge funds, do not register their shares with the SEC. This means they are not subject to the same regulatory standards that apply to mutual funds and other funds registered with the SEC.

Mutual Funds

Mutual funds are a popular way to invest in securities. Because mutual funds can offer built-in diversification and professional management, they offer certain advantages over purchasing individual stocks and bonds. But, like investing in any security, investing in a mutual fund involves certain risks, including the possibility that you may lose money.

Technically known as an "open-end company," a mutual fund is an investment company that pools money from many investors and invests it based on specific investment goals. The mutual fund raises money by selling its own shares to investors. The money is used to purchase a portfolio of stocks, bonds, short-term money-market instruments, other securities or assets, or some combination of these investments. Each share represents an ownership slice of the fund and gives the investor a proportional right, based on the number of shares he or she owns, to income and capital gains that the fund generates from its investments.

The particular investments a fund makes are determined by its objectives and, in the case of an actively managed fund, by the investment style and skill of the fund's professional manager or managers. The holdings of the mutual fund are known as its underlying investments, and the performance of those investments, minus fund fees, determine the fund's investment return.

While there are literally thousands of individual mutual funds, there are only a handful of major fund categories:

- Stock funds invest in stocks
- Bond funds invest in bonds
- Balanced funds invest in a combination of stocks and bonds

- Money market funds invest in very short-term investments and are sometimes described as cash equivalents

You can find all of the details about a mutual fund—including its investment strategy, risk profile, performance history, management, and fees—in a document called the prospectus. You should always read the prospectus before investing in a fund.

Mutual funds are equity investments, as individual stocks are. When you buy shares of a fund you become a part owner of the fund. This is true of bond funds as well as stock funds, which means there is an important distinction between owning an individual bond and owning a fund that owns the bond. When you buy a bond, you are promised a specific rate of interest and return of your principal. That's not the case with a bond fund, which owns a number of bonds with different rates and maturities. What your equity ownership of the fund provides is the right to a share of what the fund collects in interest, realizes in capital gains, and receives back if it holds a bond to maturity.

Options

Options are contracts that give the purchaser the right, but not the obligation, to buy or sell a security, such as a stock or exchange-traded fund, at a fixed price within a specific period of time.

Options can help investors manage risk. But buying and selling options also involves risk, and it is possible to lose money. It pays to learn about different types of options, trading strategies and the risks involved.

Bank Products

Banks and credit unions can provide a safe and convenient way to accumulate savings—and some banks offer services that can help you manage your money.

Deposits at banks and most credit unions are federally insured up to a limit set by Congress. And transaction (or checking) accounts and deposit accounts offer liquidity, making it easy for you to get to your funds for any reason—from day-to-day expenses to a down payment or money for unexpected emergencies. In addition to being insured by the FDIC, checking accounts let you transfer money by check or electronic payment to a person or organization that you designate as payee.

But remember, the interest you earn from bank products—including certificates of deposit (CDs)—tends to be lower than potential returns from other investments.

Types of Accounts

- Savings Accounts
- Money Market Accounts
- Certificates of Deposit (CDs)
- Federal Insurance

Real Estate

Real-estate is one of the most popular forms of investing and can certainly be used in conjunction with this course to create passive income. Joshua Kinnon of thebalance.com wrote a great article about real-estate investing and part of that is included here:

Investing in real estate is one of the oldest forms of investing, having been around since the early days of human civilization. Predating modern stock markets, real estate is one of the five basic asset classes that every investor should seriously consider adding to his or her portfolio for the unique cash flow, liquidity, profitability, tax, and diversification benefits it offers. In this introductory guide, we'll walk you through the basics of real estate investing, and discuss the different ways you might acquire or take ownership in real estate investments.

First, let's start with the basics: What is real estate investing?

What Is Real Estate Investing?

Real estate investing is a broad category of operating, investing, and financial activities centered around making money from tangible property or cash flows somehow tied to a tangible property.

There are four main ways to make money in real estate:

1. **Real Estate Appreciation**: This is when the property increases in value. This may be due to a change in the real estate market that increases demand for property in your area. It could use be due to upgrades you put into your real estate investment to make it more attractive to potential buyers or renters. Real estate appreciation is a tricky game, though.
2. **Cash Flow Income (Rent)**: This type of real estate investment focuses on buying a real estate property, such as an apartment building, and operating it so you collect a stream of cash from

rent. Cash flow income can be generated from apartment buildings, office buildings, rental houses, and more.

3. **Real Estate Related Income**: This is income generated by brokers and other industry specialists who make money through commissions from buying and selling property. It also includes real estate management companies who get to keep a percentage of rents in exchange for running the day-to-day operations of a property.

4. **Ancillary Real Estate Investment Income**: For some real estate investments, this can be a huge source of profit. Ancillary real estate investment income includes things like vending machines in office buildings or laundry facilities in low-rent apartments. In effect, they serve as mini-businesses within a bigger real estate investment, letting you make money from a semi-captive collection of customers.

The purest, simplest form of real estate investing is all about cash flow from **rents** rather than **appreciation**. Real estate investing occurs when the investor, also known as the landlord, acquires a piece of tangible property, whether that's raw farmland, land with a house on it, land with an office building on it, land with an industrial warehouse on it, or an apartment.

He or she then finds someone who wants to use this property, known as a **tenant**, and they enter into an agreement. The tenant is granted access to the real estate, to use it under certain terms, for a specific length of time, and with certain restrictions -- some of which are laid out in Federal, state, and local law, and others of which are agreed upon in the **lease contract or rental agreement**. In exchange, the tenant pays for the ability to use the real estate. The payment he or she sends to the landlord is known as "rent".

For many investors, rental income from real estate investments has a huge psychological advantage over dividends and interest from investing in stocks and bonds. They can drive by the property, see it, and touch it with their hands. They can paint it their favorite color or hire an architect and construction company to modify it. They can use their negotiation skills to determine the rental rate, allowing a good operator to generate higher *capitalization rates*, or "cap rates." (Cap rate is the net profit divided by investment cost).

From time to time, real estate investors become as misguided as stock investors during stock market bubbles, insisting that capitalization rates don't matter. Don't fall for it. If you are able to price your rental rates appropriately, you should enjoy a satisfactory rate of return on your capital after accounting for the cost of the property, including reasonable depreciation reserves, property and income taxes, maintenance, insurance, and other related expenditures. Additionally, you should measure the amount of time required to deal with the investment, as your time is the most valuable asset you have -- it's the reason passive income is so cherished by investors. (Once your holdings are large enough, you can establish or hire a real estate property management company to handle the day-to-day operations of your real estate portfolio in exchange for a percentage of the rental revenue, transforming real estate investments that had been actively managed into passive investments.)

Businesses

Starting or buying a business is also a great way to create income. There is a lot to owning or operating a business but if you do it right, you can start a business and then delegate its operation to another competent person and reap the benefits of passive income for many years to come.

For example, my friend Marc is a doctor who had a passion for pizza. So he started a pizzeria that has become very successful. Marc is now considering selling it to his partner or may consider a 9% royalty payment for the next 10 years. That means, that the work to start the payment stream has already been done and now he should be able to reap the rewards for future years without increased labor.

CHAPTER 16:
RETIREMENT INVESTING

The question isn't at what age I want to retire; it's at what income.

George Foreman

TRADITIONAL RETIREMENT INVESTING

Traditional retirement investing is when you attain a certain age and you hopefully have enough money to maintain your standard of living without having to continue to work. We look at that a bit differently in this course. We want you to work towards obtaining enough passive income to be able to retire sooner than the traditional retirement method. Nevertheless, you should know about your traditional retirement options and how tax-deferred investing can help you.

Saving for retirement, and managing income once you retire, are two important aspects of personal financial management. When it comes to saving, tax-advantaged options such as a 401(k) or IRA can be smart choices. In addition to potential tax benefits, there is an opportunity for your savings to compound over time. Once you retire, the way you manage your income can mean the difference between living comfortably in retirement and running short of money down the road. Whether you are in retirement or still saving for it, there are actions you can take now to manage retirement income. Again, we thank the folks at FINRA for putting together this information about retirement investing.

Individual Retirement Accounts (IRA)

IRA Basics

Individual retirement accounts (or IRAs) provide a way for you to set aside money for your retirement—for living expenses and to pay for the things you want to do when you have the time to do them, such as traveling or learning new skills.

Like other retirement plans, IRAs offer tax advantages—specifically, the potential for tax-deferred or tax-free growth. Tax-deferred means you postpone taxes until you withdraw money later on. Tax-free means you owe no tax on your investment earnings at all, provided you follow the rules for taking the money out of the account. But in exchange for these tax benefits, there are certain restrictions.

Here's what you need to know about IRAs.

What is an IRA?

An IRA may be either an individual retirement account you establish with a financial services company—such as a bank, brokerage firm or mutual fund company—or an individual retirement annuity that's available through an insurance company.

Certain retirement plans, including a simplified employee pension (SEP) and a SIMPLE (Savings Incentive Match Plan for Employees of Small Employers) may be set up as IRAs, though they operate a little differently from those you set up yourself. There is information about these types of plans in IRS Publication 560.

How Does an IRA Work?

Your IRA provider is the custodian for your account, investing the money as you direct and providing regular updates on your account value. Once your account is open, you can select any of the investments available through the custodian. So one key consideration in choosing a custodian is the type of investments you are planning to make.

To participate in an IRA, you must earn income, and you can contribute up to the annual limit that Congress sets. However, you can't contribute more than you earn. So, for example, if your total earned income is only $2,500 for the year, that's all you can put into an IRA, even though the contribution limit is higher.

If you're divorced, you can count alimony as earned income. And there's an exception to the earned income requirement for nonearning spouses, called a spousal IRA. This type of IRA also has contribution limits (see the Kay Bailey Hutchison Spousal IRA limit information in IRS Publication 590.)

You can put money into your IRA every year you're eligible, even if you are also enrolled in another kind of retirement savings plan through your employer. If both you and your spouse earn income, each of you can contribute to your own IRA, up to the annual limit.

Deduction Phase Out

Not everyone can deduct money they put into an IRA. Whether and how much you can deduct depends on how much you earn, and whether or not you have a retirement plan at work. The amount you can deduct begins to decrease—and ultimately phases out—when your modified adjusted gross income (AGI) reaches IRS thresholds.

All IRA contributions for a calendar year must be made in

full by the time you file your tax return for that year—typically April 15, unless that deadline falls on a weekend.

TIP: It may be smarter to spread out your contributions over the year, on a regular schedule. That way you don't have to struggle to pull together the whole amount just before the deadline, or risk putting in less than you're entitled to contribute. Another reason spreading out your contributions over the year may be smart is that it allows you to take advantage of dollar-cost averaging.

Types of IRAs

When IRAs were first introduced, there was just one basic type, which was open to anyone with earned income. But since then, IRAs have evolved to include a number of variations:

- **Traditional:** There are two categories of tax-deferred traditional IRAs: deductible and nondeductible. If you qualify to deduct your contributions, you can subtract the amount you contribute when you file your tax return for the year, reducing the income tax you owe. If you don't qualify to deduct, the contribution is made with after-tax income. The IRS website has resources to help you figure out whether, and to what extent, you can deduct your contributions.

  Earnings on investments in a traditional IRA are tax-deferred for as long as they stay in your account. When you take money out—which you can do without penalty when you turn 59½, and are required to begin doing once you turn 70½,—your withdrawal is considered regular income so you'll owe income tax on the earnings at your current rate. If you deducted your contribution, tax is due on your entire withdrawal. If you didn't, tax is due only on the portion that comes from earnings.

You can't contribute any additional amounts to a traditional IRA once you turn 70, even if you're still working.

- **Roth:** Contributions to a Roth IRA are always made with after-tax income, but the earnings are tax-free if you follow the rules for withdrawals: You must be at least 59½ and your account must have been open at least five years. What's more, with a Roth IRA you're not required to withdraw your money at any age—you can pass the entire account on to your heirs if you choose. And you can continue to contribute to a Roth as long as you have earned income, no matter how old you are. Contribution levels for a Roth are the same as those for a traditional IRA. However, there are income restrictions associated with contributing to a Roth IRA. Both you and your spouse can each establish your own Roth IRAs.

Which Is Better: Traditional or Roth IRA?

The answer to this question will vary from person to person. Assuming you're eligible to contribute to a deductible, traditional IRA or to a Roth IRA, here are some factors to consider:

- o Current-year tax benefits—Depending on your income and employment, contributions

110

to a traditional IRA may be tax deductible, which reduces your taxable income each year you contribute. But if you don't need that tax break now, a Roth IRA can give you more flexibility since you can withdraw your contributions at any time without paying taxes or fees—and you can withdraw your earnings tax-free if your account has been open at least five years and you are 59½ or older.

- o Likely future tax bracket—If you're young and likely to be in a higher tax bracket when you retire, then a Roth IRA may make more sense. But if you're likely to be in a lower tax bracket after you retire, a traditional IRA is usually the better choice. With a traditional IRA, however, you are subject to minimum required distributions when you reach age 70½.

- **Spousal:** If you're married to someone who doesn't earn income (for example, if your spouse stays home with small children), you can contribute up to the annual limit in a separate spousal IRA in that person's name as well as putting money into your own IRA. Your spouse owns the spousal IRA, chooses the investments and eventually makes the withdrawals. A spousal IRA can be a traditional deductible, traditional nondeductible or a Roth IRA, as long as you qualify for the type you select.

- **Deemed or "Sidecar" IRAs:** In some cases, you can make contributions to an IRA through your employer by taking advantage of a deemed or "sidecar" IRA provision. In this case, your employer deducts your IRA contributions from your after-tax earnings. All the rules for this account—

that is, for contribution limits, withdrawal rules and so forth—are the same as for any other IRA. If you qualify, you may be able to deduct your contribution when you file your tax return.

You might find a deemed IRA helps you to save. After all, contributions are automatic, so you don't have to remember to write a separate check to your IRA custodian and you won't be tempted to spend the money on something else. But you might also find that your choices of IRA investments are limited with this option, since they will depend on which financial services company your employer chooses as custodian or trustee of the account.

In addition, if you're not keeping accurate records of your deemed IRA contributions, you might inadvertently go over the contribution limit, which remains the same no matter how many separate IRA accounts you have. That could mean incurring penalties.

	Traditional IRA	Roth IRA
Contributions	MAY be tax deductible	Contributions are not tax deductible
	Cannot contribute past age 70 1/2	May contribute past 70 1/2
Earnings	Generally, earnings are tax deferred until withdrawn	Generally, earnings are tax deferred AND tax free upon withdrawal (*)
Income Requirements	No income limit to make contributions (deductibility can vary)	Adjusted Gross Income must be below certain limits
Distributions	Distributions required at 70 1/2	No requirement for distributions at any age during your lifetime

(*) - Unless certain requirements are not met,
in which case taxes and penalties could apply

Taking Money Out

One important thing is true of all IRAs: Taking out money early is discouraged. In fact, you generally cannot make IRA withdrawals before age 59½ without paying an early withdrawal penalty. The penalty is 10 percent of the amount you withdraw.

There are exceptions, however, if you take IRA money out to meet certain medical expenses, purchase your first home, pay college tuition bills or for certain other reasons listed in the federal tax laws. In any event, before you make any early IRA withdrawals, you should check with your tax or legal adviser to be sure you're following the rules. Even if you do not face a penalty, you will have to pay income tax on any withdrawal you make. The only exception is that you can take up to $10,000 in earnings from your Roth IRA tax-free to buy a first home for yourself or a member of your immediate family, provided you have had the Roth for at least five years.

There is a reason why withdrawing early from your IRA is made difficult. These savings vehicles are specifically designed to help you set aside money for retirement, not for other purposes. By imposing penalties for the early use of these funds, the government hopes that most people will leave their money alone. That way, the money will have time to compound, and will be available to support you in your retirement.

You should be aware, too, that unlike certain employer plans, you're not allowed to borrow against your IRA balance.

Required Withdrawals

Just as the IRA rules generally discourage you from taking your money out too early, other rules require that you begin withdrawing from a traditional IRA no later than April 1 of the year following the year in which you turn 70½. And once you do start taking money out, you must take at least your required minimum distribution, or RMD, every year. You're always free to take more than the minimum, but you must take at least that amount, or risk paying a penalty.

If you fail to keep up with your RMDs, you face a penalty that can be pretty steep: up to 50 percent of the amount you should have withdrawn but didn't, plus the income taxes you would have owed on that amount. Don't assume that if your IRA is invested in mutual funds, and you're receiving distributions from those funds, that you've automatically satisfied your RMD. It could happen, but you can't count on it.

However, if your IRA is an individual retirement annuity, which you would set up with an annuity provider such as an insurance company, your annuity provider assumes the responsibility for ensuring that the income you receive from your annuity meets your RMD.

CHAPTER 17: TOOLS, HABITS AND BEST-PRACTICES

> We are very influenced by completely automatic things that we have no control over, and we don't know we're doing it.
>
> *Daniel Kahneman*

TOOLS, HABITS AND BEST-PRACTICES

Automatic & Systematic

If you are going to do anything with consistency in life, you must make some or all elements of it systematic or automatic. Making automatic, delegating or systematizing the things that are important allow your brain to be free to focus on nuances and creativity. Creativity is where you will find your greatest success. It is not in the mundane that we get excited, but in the new and innovative aspects of life. Just imagine having to hear the same joke over and over again. Funny the first or second times but, for some reason, not very funny after that. Life is like that too.

Make things like saving into your different accounts and contributing to your retirement accounts, IRAs, maintenance and even your bill payments into automatic endeavors and you will see multiple rewards.

TIP: Be sure to set up five multiple bank accounts that flow from your main bank account where money can be automatically transferred.

Financial Experts/Team

No person is an island, they say, and it is true. We humans are each put on this Earth with individual strengths, skill sets, and even weaknesses. We are really supposed to focus on our strengths and make them better. And we should delegate our weaknesses to those who are better at them, and who thrive on doing them. For example, while I understand accounting and bookkeeping, I get a feeling of dread in my stomach when it comes to doing the work in these areas. Yes, I can do them. They are fairly straight-forward. But I would much rather pay someone who does them often and who likes to do them because I get a better quality product and everyone wins.

While you shouldn't give up your power in your wealth, you should have a team of people around you that can add strength to your team. To use a football analogy, you need a great quarterback to direct the "talent" positions, but if you do not protect the quarterback with great linemen up front, your quarterback won't be able to direct or show his strengths.

A good financial team is made up of a mix of the following people:

- Financial consultant/advisor
- Accountant
- Bookkeeper
- Attorney
- Deal analyzer
- Fund Raiser
- Insurance Agent
- …and more

Compounding

Maybe you have heard that Albert Einstein once called compound interest the "8th wonder of the world." Whether or not the crazy-looking but brilliant physicist was wowed by this amazing savings strategy is debatable, but the value of compound interest is certainly not.

What Is Compounding?

Compounding interest can be defined as "interest on interest." It means earning interest on your initial savings and then reinvesting it so you can earn interest on the new total – the original amount plus the interest. Simple interest, on the other hand, is interest paid on your initial savings only.

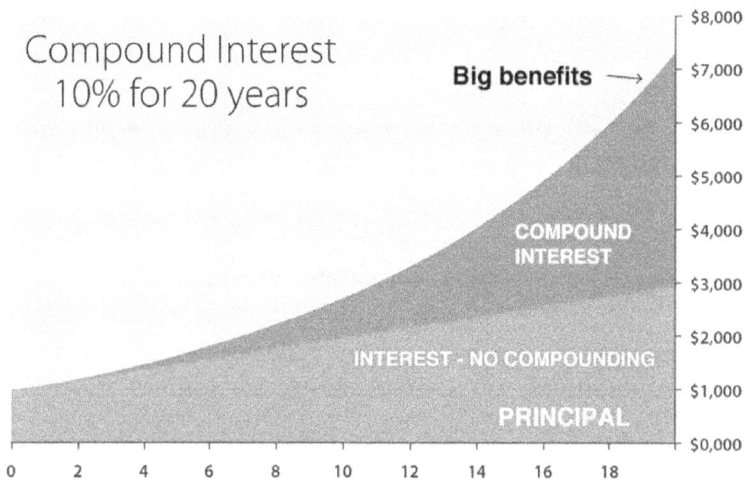

Compound Interest
10% for 20 years

Big benefits ⟶

COMPOUND INTEREST

INTEREST - NO COMPOUNDING

PRINCIPAL

Notice above how the interest "compounds" on itself and allows an exponential level of growth rather than just the geometric growth with simple interest (the middle layer).

Following is a straight-forward example of compounding on a $100,000 investment that earns a guaranteed 2.5 per cent interest. (The example assumes annual compounding and no further additions to your savings.)

Year	Value 1/1	Interest earned	Value 12/31
1	$100,000	$2,500	$102,500
2	$102,500	$2,562.50	$105,062.50
3	$105,062.50	$2,626.56	$107,689.06
10	$124,886.30	$3,122.16	$128,008.45
25	$180,872.59	$4,521.81	$185,394.41

As you can see, the longer your time horizon, the more significant the impact. It's a perfect example of how slow and steady wins the race. For comparison, the above example using a *simple interest* calculation would result in your investment growing to $162,500 over 25 years ($2,500 of interest paid each year on your principal amount without reinvesting). That falls short of the $185,394.41 after 25 years with compounding.

Of course, it's always important to think about the effects of inflation — the increase in the prices of goods and services over time — on investment returns, which can help you determine what investments are right for you. Over time, inflation reduces the purchasing power of your money.

While the above example is based on a guaranteed interest rate — something you may receive from a high-interest savings account, bond or Certificate of Deposit — compounding can apply to other investments as well. On the next graph, just look at the difference that just a few percentage points make over time. Imagine if you could earn 20%, 30% or even 40% on your investments (not uncommon if you know where to find it)!

Coumpound interests for $1000 over 40 year period
Interest rates 3%, 5%, 7%, and 10%

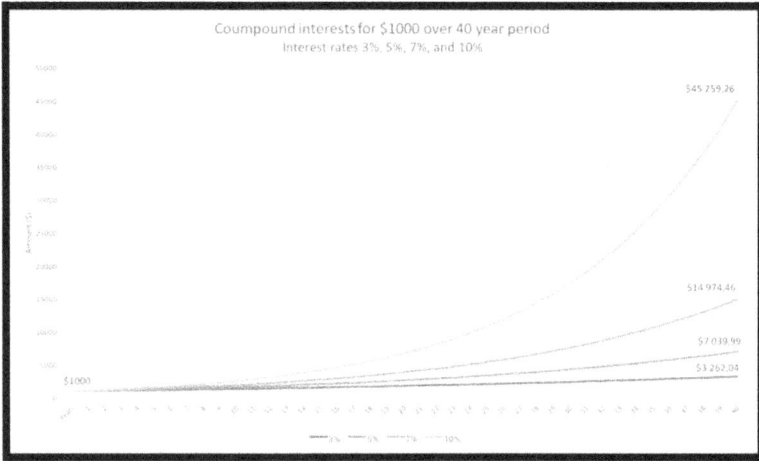

Now, here is some revealing date from a more aggressive approach:

Massive Compounding

30 Year Returns on $10,000 invested:

10% → $220,400
20% → $2,704,000
30% → $28,637,000
40% → $258,903,000

"If you aren't making 40% a year in stocks, you are doing something wrong."

William J. O'Neil – Author: How to Make Money in Stocks

Compounding Investment Income

Individual stocks, mutual funds and exchange-traded funds (ETFs) can also pay income in the form of dividends and distributions, and compounding can come into play by reinvesting those earnings.

Here's how it works. If you own a dividend-paying stock, you receive regular dividend payments. You can choose to keep that income or reinvest it to buy more shares. By reinvesting the dividend payouts, you increase the number of shares or units you own, thereby increasing your potential future dividend payouts. Think of it as earning "dividends on dividends."

Reinvesting distributions from mutual funds or ETFs that hold bonds or money-market securities can work in the same way. You can use the interest-income distributions you receive from a fund to buy more units, which would increase your future distributions because you'd own a higher number of units.

Remember, Compounding Also Works in Reverse

When your savings earn interest, you are on the *receiving* end of compound interest. But with personal debt like credit cards or car loans, it's possible to end up *paying* compounded interest. For example, if you carry a balance on your credit card, the interest you owe will compound each month. Assuming you don't make any payments, the interest owed on any balance you carry month-to-month would compound in the same way your savings did — steadily.

So, start early and invest automatically to ensure that you maximize the benefits of compounding. It is a powerful engine.

Dollar Cost Averaging

Most investors dream of "buying low and selling high." They envision buying into the market at the perfect low point, *right* before it hits an upswing, and garnering a large profit from selling at the peak. But trying to predict market highs and lows is a feat no one has ever fully mastered, despite the claims by some that they have just the right strategy that enables them to buy and sell at the most opportune times.

Attempting to predict which direction the market will go or investing merely on intuition can get you in trouble, or at the very least may cause you a great deal of frustration. One strategy that may help you navigate these investing pitfalls is dollar-cost averaging.

Dollar-cost averaging involves investing a set amount of money in an investment vehicle at regular intervals for an extended period of time, regardless of the price. Let's say you have $6,000 to invest. Instead of investing it all at once, you decide to use a dollar-cost averaging strategy and contribute $500 each month, regardless of share price, until your money is completely invested. You would end up purchasing more shares when prices are low and fewer shares when prices are high. For example, you might end up buying 20 shares when the price is low, but only 10 when the price is higher.

This strategy has the potential to reduce the risk of investing a large amount in a single investment when the cost per share is inflated. It may also help reduce the risk for an investor who tends to pull out of the market when it takes a dip, potentially causing an inopportune loss in profit.

The average cost per share may also be reduced, which has the possibility to help you gain better overall profits from the market. Utilizing a dollar-cost averaging program, the bottom line is that the average share price has the potential to be higher than your average share cost. This happens because you purchased fewer shares when the stock was priced high and more shares when the price was low. Dollar-cost averaging can also help you to avoid the annoyance and stress of continually monitoring the market in an attempt to buy and sell at "fortuitous" moments.

Dollar-cost averaging is a long-range plan, as implied by the word "averaging." In other words, the technique's best use comes only after you've stuck with it for a while, despite any nerve-racking swings in the market. When other panicky investors are scrambling to get out of the market because it has declined and to get back into it when the market has risen, you'll keep investing a specific amount based on the interval you've set.

Dollar-cost averaging does not ensure a profit in rising markets or protect against a loss in declining markets. This type of investment program involves continuous investment in securities regardless of the fluctuating price levels of such securities. Investors should consider their financial ability to continue making purchases through periods of low and high price levels. The return and principal value of stocks fluctuate with changes in market conditions. Shares, when sold, may be worth more or less than their original cost.

So, if you believe in statistics such as "the market has returned around 10% for the past 100 years," then you should consider this unemotional strategy. Just be aware that sometimes there are long periods where things do NOT go up, maybe even periods of several years. You will have to sit through those periods (if you have the time and stomach for it) and hope that the statistics will be "true this time."

Diversification or Di-*worse*-ification

Practically every investment has some kind of risk associated with it. The stock market rises and falls. An increase in interest rates can cause a decline in the bond market. No matter what you decide to invest in, risk is something you have to consider.

One key to successful investing is managing risk while maintaining the potential for good returns on your investments. One of the most effective ways to help manage your investment risk is to diversify (or is it?). Diversification is an investment strategy aimed at managing risk by spreading your money across a variety of investments such as stocks, bonds, real estate, and cash alternatives; but diversification certainly does not guarantee a profit or protect against loss.

The main philosophy behind diversification is simple: "Don't put all your eggs in one basket." Spreading the risk among a number of different investment categories, as well as over several different industries, can help offset a loss in any one investment.

Likewise, the power of diversification may help smooth your returns over time. As one investment increases, it may offset the decreases in another. This may allow your portfolio to ride out market fluctuations, providing a more steady performance under various economic conditions. By potentially reducing the impact of market ups and downs, diversification could go far in enhancing your comfort level with investing.

Diversification is one of the main reasons why mutual funds may be so attractive for both experienced and novice investors. Many individual investors have a limited investment budget and may find it challenging to construct a portfolio that is sufficiently diversified.

For a modest initial investment, you can purchase shares in a diversified portfolio of securities. You have "built-in" diversification. Depending on the objectives of the fund, it may contain a variety of stocks, bonds, and cash vehicles, or a combination of them.

Whether you are investing in mutual funds or are putting together your own combination of stocks, bonds, and other investment vehicles, it is a good idea to keep in mind the concept of diversifying. The value of stocks, bonds, and mutual funds fluctuate with market conditions. When it is time to sell your investment, it may be worth more or less than their original cost.

But wait a minute! Diversification is preached by so many investment gurus as "the free lunch" in investing. And if you are going to play it safe, it probably is a good way to go about it. However, it will also take great investments and average them with poor investments, thereby making your investments get an "average" return. I don't know about you, but I don't wake up every day wishing I was average. I strive for excellence.

Now I am not saying that you shouldn't diversify. In fact, you should. I am saying that it isn't the panacea that Wall Street, lawyers or your CPA may advise you that it is.

Consider this. In 2014, the S&P 500 made a 14.1% return. Now, the S&P500 index is made up of the 500 most followed companies traded in the United States. You would know most of them. Microsoft, Apple, Netflix, Exxon, US Steel, ATT and others are all components of the index. However, the index is comprised of all 500 stocks. So if you have some great performers in there, their performance will be brought down by the lousy performers in the index. In other words, not all companies do well at the same time and certainly all of their stocks don't perform well at the same time. Further, if you looked at the top 10 best-performing stocks in the index, and only invested in them, you would have returned a whopping 185% return!

So you get to decide if diversification is right for you. Does diversification help or make things "worse?"

I'll give you a guideline:

Diversify AMONG Asset Classes;
Concentrate WITHIN Asset Classes.

In other words, if you are in the stock market, work to become an expert in a few "super-performers" rather than mixing those super-performers with under-performers. If you are in real-estate, learn one area of real-estate really well. For example become an expert in residential rentals rather than rentals plus land speculation plus strip malls plus house flipping. These are all sciences unto themselves and like investments if you don't concentrate to become excellent in one or two areas, you will become average in many.

And if you choose to diversify, then have some real-estate, some stocks, some bonds, some gold, etc.

Investment Bathtubs

Some people call them buckets. In some of our courses, we call them Investment Bathtubs. They are really just "accounts." The concept is simple: take your extra savings and fill up one bathtub first, say your emergency bathtub. Let's say that you are looking for 3 to 6 months of Sleep Money or rainy day funds that will support you if you lose your income. You will build this amount up first. Then, once those funds are built up, you have filled the first investment bathtub, let the excess flow into another bathtub for retirement or stocks. You could also start with a debt bathtub that you use to pay off debt. This is a great way to systematically start your investment habits so that you don't have to do much thinking.

Deferred Gratification

So, what is an important component to financial success?

You could argue that the key is getting enough marketable skills to be able to get a job and earn a decent income. Or that the key is to consistently track your monthly spending in a budget spreadsheet. Or you could even argue the key is to learn the ins and outs of investing.

But really, while all of these things are very important to your long-term financial health, each of them is based on upon one particular characteristic: the ability to delay gratification. Almost above all else, I would argue that it's the ability to carry out delayed gratification that is the true key to financial success.

The problem with most people in Western societies is that we are so affluent. What? Let me explain. Because of our programming, we are always wanting more, and that's OK. It's just that more often means things: more expensive things, bigger things, things that are fancier. We get seduced by nicer cars, even if we have a perfectly good 3 year old car. We are tempted to buy a nicer house, in a nicer neighborhood. We are honored by the offer to join the country club. We think we need a Louis Vitton purse. So, what do we do when we get a raise, a bonus or earn more money? We spend it on often unnecessary lifestyle items. Rather, we should spend it on things that can help us earn money. We sacrifice our future so that we can pursue our present. So, many of us in Western society, even will all of our abundance, are broke, or unhappy, or worse.

While many external factors can cause financial hardship, one of the common internal factors that can result in financial difficulty is an inability to appreciate delayed gratification. If you're buried under debt, struggling to pay your car loan, or even having trouble paying your mortgage, then it's possible you might benefit from a different perspective on long-term goals.

We must learn to delay gratification until we can no longer delay gratification. That means that we keep our standard of living the same for a while, and then later jump up to a much higher level that we can afford and get used to that for a while.

Ownership: Rent vs. Buy

John Rockefeller said, "Own nothing but control everything." One of the richest men of all time, Rockefeller knew that it wasn't all about ownership. It was about use. When you get down to it, we are all just renting our things (and our time) while we are here on Earth. When we die, we leave with nothing, just like we arrived.

If you really sit down and do the math, you will often see that there are huge benefits to renting rather than owning. Let's do an example. Let's say that you want to buy a $200,000 modest home in a nice neighborhood. You may need to borrow $150,000 to buy it with a 5% mortgage. That means that your payments are roughly $800 per month. Taxes are $300 per month. That is about $1,100 per month so far. But there is also maintenance: roofs, air conditioners, appliances, are just the big ones. You also must pay the yard guy (or do it yourself), paint the rooms occasionally, and replace windows and other things from time to time. But let's just take an average of all of that and call it deferred maintenance of $400 per month. So, now you are up to around $1500 per month.

Using the information I found on Zillow, you would pay rent of around $1,000 per month for a similar home in the same neighborhood. Certainly less. But of course you give up the chance for price appreciation and having the exact cabinets you want in the kitchen. But now, what happens if the roof leaks and needs to be replaced? Well, you just pick up the phone and call the owner and she must replace the roof for twenty- or twenty-five thousand dollars; NOT you. Most people don't do the numbers on home ownership; they just believe that it is the "smart" thing to do. Often it is, but what if you want to move? Well, you have to prepare the house; stage the house; repair any deferred items, etc.; and then you have to pay a real-estate agent 6% of your price to sell it and that is IF you can get the price that you want. Plus, all of this takes time. Just know that there are benefits to owning, but there are benefits to renting as well.

The same is true of cars, boats, airplanes, and even fancy clothing. Ownership simply means that you must maintain the item (cost) while rental usually means that someone else pays for the maintenance.

Watch Who You Get Advice From

As you embark on your journey to becoming an Epic Millionaire, you will find many people who, out of love or significance, will want to give you advice. Sometimes that advice is good and provided with the best intentions. But often, it is just wrong. Just be careful who you take your advice from. Have they done it? Have they made the mistakes along the way? Do they have disempowering beliefs that may actually hinder your progress?

A school-teacher that makes $40,000 per year is probably not the best person to advise you on accounting strategies for passive income real-estate. A doctor is probably not the best person to tell you how to run your restaurant. Your plumber is probably not a great source for stock-trading advice.

You should certainly seek advice along your journey. No doubt about it. Just amass that advice and make your own decision, but certainly give more weight to someone who has actually walked the walk.

Say "No" More

One of the critical factors that studies of millionaires show to be a key to success is the ability to stay focused. You are going to be distracted along the way and offered a growing number of "opportunities" as you grow. The trick is to not be tempted by most of them. Stay the course. Stay focused. That means that you will have to say "no" more. No to things that are not on your path. No to distractions. No to bad habits. The more you say "no," the more time that you will make for the "yesses" in your life.

Celebrate

Remember to celebrate your wins along the way. By celebrating, you tell yourself that it is OK to sacrifice; to strive; to work; to be disciplined; and to succeed. That way, the next time, you will already be conditioned. Set your goal for success, but when you do, remember to set your celebration goal too. Treat yourself to a nice massage. Take your spouse out to a nice dinner if you hit a milestone. Celebrate! Enjoy! That is what life is all about. It is not simply the destination that we are after, but the journey along the way. Let's enjoy it all.

Risk vs. Reward

Just know that you need to take prudent risks in order to reap rewards. Sure, you can bury your money in your backyard, but you will lose buying power to inflation (bread will cost more next year than it does today). You will get a return OF your money if you put it in the bank earning 1%. But you must pay tax on the 1% and you will lose 2% to inflation. So again, the no-risk strategy of being safe is actually a negative reward. On the other hand, you could put your money into a penny stocks and buy 100,000 shares for 2 cents or $2,000 which could pay off wildly if the company succeeds turning your investment into $1-million. But the chances are you may lose it all. In every strategy there is a reward to risk component, and you should become proficient at determining it before you get involved in an investment. The wealthy always know their downside and have calculated for it. You should too. The general rule is (within reason) the higher the potential risk, the higher the potential reward.

PASSIVE INCOME

Before, we get into customizing your own investment blueprint, we need to talk about passive income. In fact, this whole course has been geared to getting you to see the benefits of replacing your earned income with passive income – so you obtain Financial Freedom. We discussed briefly what passive income is, but let's delve into a few different kinds of passive income that most wealth people use, and have used, to accelerate their financial abundance.

A quick note: you don't need to do all of these. You should probably just find one, or maybe two, categories of passive income that may be interesting and fun for you and become a passionate expert in it or them. The most common form of passive income for many people is real estate. But real-estate may not be your game. It took me a few years to realize it. I understand it, but it is not my game. The stock market is more my speed. For some of my friends, the short-term rental market is for them. Many of my friends have set up their own businesses. Still others are successful selling on Amazon or have their own online courses.

I have one friend that has set his whole life up to be an example of financial freedom. His name is Sotiris and he lives in Greece. Sotiris is 62, but for many years, he has lived from the income that he created from his own passive income streams. He works pretty hard for a few months, setting up his next passive income stream, and then relaxes while the income comes in. He is like a rocket, spending huge amounts of energy to get off the ground, but once he

134

is in orbit, he stays there nearly effortlessly. For example, about 10 years ago, when the solar business was booming in Greece, Sotiris saw an opportunity. He figured out a way to invest in setting up his own 1 Megawatt solar farm on some family land. Today, I he makes about $60,000 per year from his solar business. But the beauty is, his panels just sit in the sun and make power and the power company sends him a check every quarter. On some other land, he grows organic olives and oranges. Last year, Sotiris set up a business where he rents BMW motorcycles and gives tours to foreigners who want to explore Greece. He interviewed several people and found a partner who will handle all of the details: the bookings, the tours, the motorcycle maintenance, the accounting, everything. Sotiris provides advice to his partner and reaps the rewards as long as the business is successful. He also owns or has owned bars, parking garages and filling stations all run by partners or employees.

Today, he rents a 5 bedroom condominium in one of the nicest areas of Athens and spends most of his time traveling, taking motorcycle trips, and plotting his next passive income idea. To me, he is a model of how one should set up a successful financial life.

While this isn't intended to be a course in passive income, it is a concept upon which this whole financial freedom theory is based. You should become passionate about some of the ways that passive income can help you, and if you need, we can steer you to some resources and partners that are experts in many areas.

So what is it going to be for you?

More Passive Income Ideas

Here are some ideas for generating passive income and I know that we have mentioned many of these before, but I like to keep the ideas top-of-mind for you.

- Dividend Stocks
- Peer to Peer Lending
- Rental Properties
- Annuities
- Invest Automatically In The Stock Market
- Refinance Your Mortgage
- Invest In A Business
- Sell an eBook or Audio Book Online
- Create a Course
- Selling Stock Photos and Videos
- Licensing Music
- Create an App
- Affiliate Marketing
- Design T-Shirts, Hats and Cups
- Sell Digital Files on Etsy
- List Your Place On Airbnb
- Create and AirBnB rental business
- Car Wash
- Rent Out Your Car
- Operate a Parking Garage
- Vending Machines
- Storage Rentals
- Laundromat
- Cashback Rewards Cards
- Cashback Sites
- Develop An App
- High Yield Savings Accounts And Money Market Funds

- CD Ladders
- Invest In A REIT (Real Estate Investment Trust)

Laura MacArthur wrote a great blog on Vcita.com that discusses some passive income ideas that you may wish to explore. Here is an excerpt:

Dividend Stocks

Dividends are profits paid to those who own stock in a company.

To calculate a dividend yield, divide the amount the company pays in dividends each year by the stock price. If a stock pays annual dividends of $1.00 per share and trades at $10, the yield is 10%.

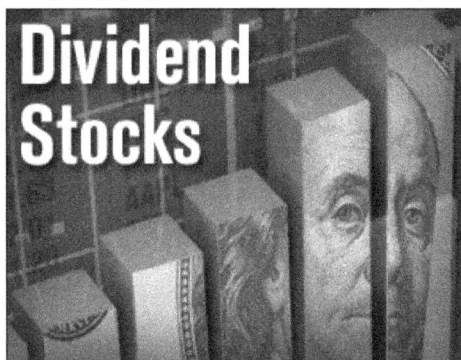

When you invest in a business that schedules its dividend payments, the money can become a reasonably reliable source of income, but bear in mind that stocks with higher dividend yields involve risk and can drop in value. The best strategy is to hold them for a long time after buying: don't over-react to sudden market changes.

Real Estate

Real estate investing is another popular source of passive income. You can buy or rent a property, make it available as an Airbnb and, depending on where you're located, earn up to $10,000 per month. (According to Fundera, the average Airbnb host makes $924 a month.) The initial financial outlay will also vary according to location: one host estimated that a one-bedroom unit in Silicon Valley cost between $6,000 and $7,000 to set up.

Once you've gotten everything ready, the only demand on your time will be trips to the grocery store (to stock up on water and coffee) or laundromat to keep towels and linens fresh for guests. If your work and family commitments require you to be as hands-off as possible, there are several companies that let you invest in commercial and residential real estate projects without assuming the burdens of ownership:

- **DiversyFund:** This private real estate investment trust allows you to passively invest in lower risk multifamily housing for as little as $500. Preferred returns for their properties average around 7%.
- **Rich Uncles:** A popular crowdfunded real estate investment company, Rich Uncles lets you invest as little as $5.00, making it a perfect introductory platform for those who are new to real estate.

Businesses

Investing in a business can be highly risky, but there is also the potential for high returns. Many of those who invested in Uber and Houzz at the beginning are super-wealthy today. Most businesses fail, so unless you are willing to work very hard in the beginning, or have a partner who will, be prepared for some tough times. However, you don't have to be the one to fail. Just be passionate, understand business, and hire the right talent. You will have the ability to hand it off in no time.

Peer to Peer Lending:

Peer-to-peer lending platforms like the Lending Club match lenders with borrowers.

You can invest in different kinds of loans (each of which involves its own risk level and return) and receive a passive income when the borrower makes payments. Single loan investments are available for as little as $25, so you can reduce risk exposure by investing small amounts in several different loans.

If you prefer to devote time instead of money, there are several passive income options available. Some require more time to set up and maintain while others involve a single action that triggers a recurring revenue stream.

Vending Machines

Vending machine franchises are an appealing microbusiness because of the low overhead and minimal startup costs (as little as $150 per machine plus inventory).

Depending on what you're selling and the location of the machine, Vendsoft estimates that you can make anywhere from $5.00 to over $100 per week.

The real investment is in terms of time, as some machines need to be regularly restocked. If you're pressed for time, go with products that aren't perishable, such as toys and trinkets.

Affiliate Marketing

Affiliate marketing is nearly as old as the Internet itself. When you are an affiliate, you get a commission on every sale of a product or service that you recommend. There's no need to create and sell anything yourself: all you have to do is sign up, get a unique tracking link, and insert it in your blog posts or YouTube videos.

If you're willing to put some extra time into it, the payoffs can be impressive: solopreneur Michelle Schroeder-Gardner of Making Sense of Cents reported that her blog produces affiliate income of $50,000 per month. Others report returns that are a lot more modest but still regular.

Many companies that do business online offer an affiliate program, and each one has different payment terms. Below are some of the more popular opportunities:

- **Amazon Associates:** Who doesn't love Amazon? It's a massive online marketplace that delivers everything from socks and candy to MacBook Pros and Alexa home systems within a day. You can earn up to 10% on any qualifying sale through your link.
- **YouTube Partner Program**: If you already have a YouTube channel, you can monetize it if you have at least 1,000 subscribers and 4,000 watch hours in the previous 12 months. YouTube takes in an average of $7.60 per 1,000 ad views and shares 55% of this revenue with video creators, which amounts to roughly $4.18 for every 1,000 views.

It's not a lot, but once a video is monetized, it can keep earning for you.

- **ClickBank:** Unlike traditional affiliate networks, Clickbank is a marketplace for both digital product sellers and affiliates. When you sign up, you get a unique affiliate link for the products you want to advertise. Place it on your blog or website and when people click through to the vendor's site and buy, you receive a commission. Most products pay a commission of 70% and up, so if you sell a $100 product, you will get $70. Warren Wheeler of AMNinjas wrote a case study about <u>one marketer who earned $300 a day</u>.

Display or CPC Ads

Like affiliate marketing, making money from display and CPC ads require you to have an online presence like a website or blog.

With display ads (also known as CPM ads), you received a fixed amount of money based on how many people view them. In general, you get paid for a thousand impressions. Cost-Per-Click (CPC) ads are inserted in your sidebar or content, and you get paid every time visitors click on them.
How much you make depends primarily on your site traffic, so this passive income type is best-suited to bloggers with a healthy following.

Some companies also pay more per view or per click than others. Google AdSense is the best-known ad networking platform. You sign up for an account and link it to your blog. Google will automatically display ads in your posts and whenever a visitor clicks on them, you will be paid.

Drop Shipping

With drop shipping, you can start a business with little to no money.

After opening an online store, you work with a drop shipper to deliver products to buyers. You don't stock anything yourself: instead, you transfer order and shipment information to a wholesaler, manufacturer, or other retailer, and they send the goods. You only pay when the customer does, so you're never on the hook financially.

One of the biggest appeals of drop shipping (other than the nonexistent startup cost) is that it's easy to scale your business based on demand. When the holidays roll around, scaling up to meet higher sales volumes is easy.

Profit margins depend on what you're selling. More expensive items could earn you 5 to 10% per sale while lower-ticket purchases can yield a 100% margin. On average, gross margins appear to be 10% to 15%.

The easiest way to start a drop shipping business is sign up for a Shopify account and add the Oberlo app, which is Shopify's integrated drop shipping supplier network. You use it to find popular products to sell, add them to your Shopify store, and fulfill all orders.

Selling Stock Photos

If you're a professional photographer (or just REALLY good with a camera), you can upload a portfolio to a stock photography website and make money every time someone downloads any of your images. Commission rates and payment structures will vary from one website to the next, but popular platforms that are worth investigating include:

- **Shutterstock:** Every time one of your images is downloaded, Shutterstock will initially pay 25 cents. When sales reach the $500 mark, payment is raised to 33 cents. Once you reach lifetime earnings of $10,000, you earn 38 cents per download.
- **Fotolia:** Fotolia, which was recently purchased by Adobe Stock, has two pricing models. You earn a commission of 20% to 63% on photos sold to customers using a Pay-As-You-Go plan while commission on sales to Subscription customers is 33%.
- **iStock:** iStock has different commission rates depending on whether your photos appear anywhere else. Exclusive images start at 25% per download while nonexclusive ones are capped at 15%.

Create a Udemy course

Udemy is an online learning platform that over 130,000 courses taught by more than 42,000 instructors. If you have a special skill, proficiency, or professional qualification, you can make money teaching what you know to the millions of students seeking to improve their knowledge.

After signing up for an instructor account, you will have to build your course by recording a video. If you are a professional or even amateur videographer, this part won't be too hard. If not, you may have to invest in professional support, but once your video assets are created, you're all set.

Sell an eBook

If you have a great idea and the ability to write about it, you can earn passive income by selling eBooks.

Amazon Createspace is the most popular self-publishing platform because it's so easy to use. There are templates for both print and digital books, so you're not as likely to make formatting mistakes, and if you're not artistically inclined, you can use one of the many modifiable cover templates.

EBook publishing is one of those income sources that generate revenue long after your book appears in the Amazon marketplace. You can set your own price, which Amazon will augment to recoup any costs. It charges 15 cents per MB of your eBook size if you're selling it for anywhere between $2.99 and $9.99, and delivery fees will vary from one country to the next. Books priced below or above this range don't incur a delivery fee.

The important thing is to pick one. Then, read a book, take a course, get a mentor, do something....but most importantly: Just Start! It won't happen until you take action. Passive income is your key to becoming an Epic Millionaire, but you must take action.

Oh, and don't get bogged down by the million reasons that you are going to come up with about why or how you CANNOT do it. Your brain will try to protect you, as will many of those around you. Where will I get the money? I don't have the time? What if I fail? I don't know anything about that business!..... and on and on. Just know that every negative thought or question can be overcome with realistic ability, knowledge, and attitude.

Now, it's up to you to decide. If you can't decide, then we recommend that you start with real-estate. Figure out a way to buy a house and rent it out (you may have to find people who will lend you money or will mentor you in the process).

CHAPTER 18: DESIGN YOUR TRACK

DESIGN YOUR TRACK

In a moment, we will design your very own plan. But first we need some assumptions in order to move forward. Answer the following questions to design your investment blueprint.

What is your combined, after-tax income (monthly):

_____

Now allocate each payment of that amount into the 5 categories we discussed earlier:

PYF	Lifestyle	Fun	Education	Tithing/NE

What are the year-end amounts you will have invested in each account:

PYF	Lifestyle	Fun	Education	Tithing/NE

What Passive Income investment(s) are you deciding to make, what field or what specifically:

_____

_____

_____

What Return on Investment (ROI) are you targeting:

_____

_____

_____

_____

Please see the Model Blueprints that follow to get an idea of how this will all work for you.

If you need more help or resources, send an email to: blueprint@hackingmoney.com

CHAPTER 19: MODEL INVESTMENT BLUEPRINTS

Mo

del

Invest

ment

Bluep

rints

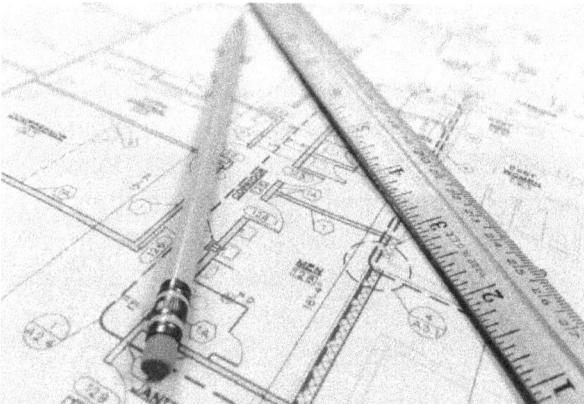

In the following pages, we show you 6-year plans of what it would look like if you set up your 5 bank accounts and contribute diligently to them in the amounts that we recommend from your after-tax income. Then, you take your savings from your Pay Yourself First (PYF) account and invest it into cash-flowing assets starting in year 2. In these examples, our passive income is primarily real-estate and we also get some great leverage from real-estate. But it can be any passive income business. We make assumptions regarding your Asset (net) ROI, down payment on asset purchases, and the asset appreciation rate. We don't factor in debt or taxes in these calculations. It is your job to get taxes reduced as low as possible. We also take your income from those assets and use it to purchase an additional cash flowing asset the next year and use those combined incomes to continue asset purchases.

Click here to watch the explainer video about how this works:

http://www.HackingMoney.com/blueprint

Notice the following:
- how quickly your net worth goes up in the last column
- when you can replace your earned income (salary) with Passive income (quit your job)
- you can begin to increase your standard of living expenses as your Passive Income increases, but it is better to use the delayed gratification concept to increase your living expenses once you have significantly increased your Passive Income.
- To do your own calculations, please go to: http://www.HackingMoney.com/spreadsheet

Investment Blueprint

Aggressive Real Estate

Assumptions:

Income (after tax): $ **50,000** (no consumer debt)

Net ROI on Asset: 15%

Downpmt on Asset: 20%

Asset appreciation rate: 5%

end of Year	20% PYF*	50% Liv'g XP	10% Education	10% Fun	10% Tithe/NE	1st Asset Value	1st Asset Income	2nd Asset Value	2nd Asset Income	3rd Asset Value	3rd Asset Income	4th Asset Value	4th Asset Income	5th Asset Value	5th Asset Income	Assets Controlled	Net Worth
1	$ 10,000	$ 25,000	$ 5,000	$ 5,000	$ 5,000											$ 10,000	$ 10,000
2	$ 20,000	$ 25,000	$ 5,000	$ 5,000	$ 5,000											$ 100,000	$ 20,000
2 (after asset purchase)						$100,000	$ 15,000										
3	$ 25,000	$ 25,000	$ 5,000	$ 5,000	$ 5,000	$105,000	$ 15,750	$125,000	$ 18,750							$ 230,000	$ 46,000
3 (after asset purchase)																	
4	$ 44,500	$ 25,000	$ 5,000	$ 5,000	$ 5,000	$110,250	$ 16,538	$131,250	$ 19,688	$ 222,500	$ 33,375					$ 464,000	$ 92,800
4 (after asset purchase)																	
5	$ 79,600	$ 25,000	$ 5,000	$ 5,000	$ 5,000	$115,763	$ 17,364	$137,813	$ 20,672	$ 233,625	$ 35,044	$ 398,000	$ 59,700			$ 885,200	$ 177,040
5 (after asset purchase)																	
6	$ 142,780	$ 25,000	$ 5,000	$ 5,000	$ 5,000	$121,551	$ 18,233	$144,703	$ 21,705	$ 245,306	$ 36,796	$ 417,900	$ 62,685	$ 713,500	$ 107,085	$ 1,643,360	$ 328,672
6 (after asset purchase)																	

*PYF income is determined by adding contribution amount to asset income amount(s)

Investment Blueprint

Aggressive Real Estate

153

Assumptions:

Income (after tax): $ 100,000 (no consumer debt)

Net ROI on Asset: 15%

Downpmt on Asset: 20%

Asset appreciation rate: 5%

	Bank Accounts					Asset Accounts										Summary	
end of Year	20% PYF*	50% Livg XP	10% Education	10% Fun	10% Tithe/NE	1st Asset Value	1st Asset Income	2nd Asset Value	2nd Asset Income	3rd Asset Value	3rd Asset Income	4th Asset Value	4th Asset Income	5th Asset Value	5th Asset Income	Assets Controlled	Net Worth
1	$ 20,000	$ 50,000	$ 10,000	$ 10,000	$ 10,000											$ 20,000	$ 20,000
2	$ 40,000	$ 50,000	$ 10,000	$ 10,000	$ 10,000												
2 (after asset purchase)						$200,000	$ 30,000									$ 200,000	$ 40,000
3	$ 50,000	$ 50,000	$ 10,000	$ 10,000	$ 10,000												
3 (after asset purchase)						$210,000	$ 31,500	$250,000	$ 37,500							$ 460,000	$ 92,000
4	$ 89,000	$ 50,000	$ 10,000	$ 10,000	$ 10,000												
4 (after asset purchase)						$220,500	$ 33,075	$262,500	$ 39,375	$ 445,000	$ 66,750					$ 928,000	$ 185,600
5	$ 159,200	$ 50,000	$ 10,000	$ 10,000	$ 10,000												
5 (after asset purchase)						$231,525	$ 34,729	$275,625	$ 41,344	$ 467,250	$ 70,088	$796,000	$119,400			$1,770,400	$ 354,080
6	$ 285,560	$ 50,000	$ 10,000	$ 10,000	$ 10,000												
6 (after asset purchase)						$243,101	$ 36,465	$289,406	$ 43,411	$ 490,613	$ 73,592	$835,800	$125,370	$1,427,800	$ 214,170	$3,286,720	$ 657,344

*PYF income is determined by adding contribution amount to asset income amount(s)

Investment Blueprint

Moderate Real Estate

Assumptions:

Income (after tax): $ **50,000** (no consumer debt)

Net ROI on Asset: 10%

Downpmt on Asset: 20%

Asset appreciation rate: 5%

end of	Bank Accounts					Asset Accounts										Summary	
	20%	50%	10%	10%	10%	1st Asset		2nd Asset		3rd Asset		4th Asset		5th Asset		Assets	Net
Year	PYF*	Livg.XP	Education	Fun	Tithe/NE	Value	Income	Value	Income	Value	Income	Value	Income	Value	Income	Controlled	Worth
1	$ 10,000	$ 25,000	$ 5,000	$ 5,000	$ 5,000											$ 10,000	$ 10,000
2	$ 20,000	$ 25,000	$ 5,000	$ 5,000	$ 5,000											$ 100,000	$ 20,000
(after asset purchase) 2						$100,000	$ 10,000										
3	$ 20,000	$ 25,000	$ 5,000	$ 5,000	$ 5,000											$ 205,000	$ 41,000
(after asset purchase) 3						$105,000	$ 10,500	$100,000	$ 10,000								
4	$ 30,500	$ 25,000	$ 5,000	$ 5,000	$ 5,000											$ 367,750	$ 73,550
(after asset purchase) 4						$110,250	$ 11,025	$105,000	$ 10,500	$152,500	$ 15,250						
5	$ 46,775	$ 25,000	$ 5,000	$ 5,000	$ 5,000											$ 620,013	$ 124,003
(after asset purchase) 5						$115,763	$ 11,576	$110,250	$ 11,025	$160,125	$ 16,013	$ 233,875	$ 23,388				
6	$ 72,001	$ 25,000	$ 5,000	$ 5,000	$ 5,000											$ 1,011,019	$ 202,204
(after asset purchase) 6						$121,551	$ 12,155	$115,763	$ 11,576	$168,131	$ 16,813	$ 245,569	$ 24,557	$ 360,006	$ 36,001		

*PYF income is determined by adding contribution amount to asset income amount(s)

154

Investment Blueprint

Assumptions:

Income (after tax): $ 100,000 (no consumer debt)

Net ROI on Asset: 10%

Downpmt on Asset: 20%

Asset appreciation rate: 5%

Moderate Real Estate

end of Year	20% PYF*	50% Livg XP	10% Education	10% Fun	10% Tithe/NE	1st Asset Value	1st Asset Income	2nd Asset Value	2nd Asset Income	3rd Asset Value	3rd Asset Income	4th Asset Value	4th Asset Income	5th Asset Value	5th Asset Income	Assets Controlled	Net Worth
1	$ 20,000	$ 50,000	$ 10,000	$ 10,000	$ 10,000											$ 20,000	$ 20,000
2	$ 40,000	$ 50,000	$ 10,000	$ 10,000	$ 10,000											$ 200,000	$ 40,000
(after asset purchase)						$200,000	$ 20,000										
3	$ 40,000	$ 50,000	$ 10,000	$ 10,000	$ 10,000	$210,000	$ 21,000	$200,000	$ 20,000							$ 410,000	$ 82,000
(after asset purchase)																	
4	$ 61,000	$ 50,000	$ 10,000	$ 10,000	$ 10,000	$220,500	$ 22,050	$210,000	$ 21,000	$305,000	$ 30,500					$ 735,500	$ 147,100
(after asset purchase)																	
5	$ 93,550	$ 50,000	$ 10,000	$ 10,000	$ 10,000	$231,525	$ 23,153	$220,500	$ 22,050	$320,250	$ 32,025	$467,750	$ 46,775			$ 1,240,025	$ 248,005
(after asset purchase)																	
6	$ 144,003	$ 50,000	$ 10,000	$ 10,000	$ 10,000	$243,101	$ 24,310	$231,525	$ 23,153	$336,263	$ 33,626	$491,138	$ 49,114	$ 720,013	$ 72,001	$ 2,022,039	$ 404,408
(after asset purchase)																	

*PYF income is determined by adding contribution amount to asset income amount(s)

Investment Blueprint

Conservative Real Estate

Assumptions:

Income (after tax): $ 50,000 (no consumer debt)
Net ROI on Asset: 6%
Downpmt on Asset: 20%
Asset appreciation rate: 5%

	Bank Accounts					Asset Accounts										Summary	
end of Year	20% PYF*	50% Livg XP	10% Education	10% Fun	10% Tithe/NE	1st Asset Value	1st Asset Income	2nd Asset Value	2nd Asset Income	3rd Asset Value	3rd Asset Income	4th Asset Value	4th Asset Income	5th Asset Value	5th Asset Income	Assets Controlled	Net Worth
1	$ 10,000	$ 25,000	$ 5,000	$ 5,000	$ 5,000											$ 10,000	$ 10,000
2	$ 20,000	$ 25,000	$ 5,000	$ 5,000	$ 5,000											$ 100,000	$ 20,000
2 (after asset purchase)						$100,000	$ 6,000										
3	$ 16,000	$ 25,000	$ 5,000	$ 5,000	$ 5,000											$ 165,000	$ 37,000
3 (after asset purchase)						$105,000	$ 6,300	$ 80,000	$ 4,800								
4	$ 21,100	$ 25,000	$ 5,000	$ 5,000	$ 5,000											$ 299,750	$ 59,950
4 (after asset purchase)						$110,250	$ 6,615	$ 84,000	$ 5,040	$ 105,500	$ 6,330						
5	$ 27,985	$ 25,000	$ 5,000	$ 5,000	$ 5,000											$ 454,663	$ 90,933
5 (after asset purchase)						$115,763	$ 6,946	$ 88,200	$ 5,292	$ 110,775	$ 6,647	$ 139,925	$ 8,396				
6	$ 37,280	$ 25,000	$ 5,000	$ 5,000	$ 5,000											$ 663,794	$ 132,759
6 (after asset purchase)						$121,551	$ 7,293	$ 92,610	$ 5,557	$ 116,314	$ 6,979	$ 146,921	$ 8,815	$ 186,399	$ 11,184		

*PYF income is determined by adding contribution amount to asset income amount(s)

156

Investment Blueprint

Conservative Real Estate

Assumptions:
Income (after tax): $ 100,000 (no consumer debt)
Net ROI on Asset: 6%
Downpmt on Asset: 20%
Asset appreciation rate: 5%

end of Year	Bank Accounts 20% PYF*	50% Livg XP	10% Education	10% Fun	10% Tithe/NE	1st Asset Value	1st Asset Income	2nd Asset Value	2nd Asset Income	3rd Asset Value	3rd Asset Income	4th Asset Value	4th Asset Income	5th Asset Value	5th Asset Income	Assets Controlled	Net Worth
1	$ 20,000	$ 50,000	$ 10,000	$ 10,000	$ 10,000											$ 20,000	$ 20,000
2	$ 40,000	$ 50,000	$ 10,000	$ 10,000	$ 10,000											$ 200,000	$ 40,000
(after asset purchase)						$200,000	$ 12,000										
3	$ 32,000	$ 50,000	$ 10,000	$ 10,000	$ 10,000	$210,000	$ 12,000	$160,000	$ 9,600							$ 370,000	$ 74,000
(after asset purchase)																	
4	$ 42,200	$ 50,000	$ 10,000	$ 10,000	$ 10,000	$220,500	$ 13,230	$168,000	$ 10,080	$ 211,000	$ 12,660					$ 599,500	$ 119,900
(after asset purchase)																	
5	$ 55,970	$ 50,000	$ 10,000	$ 10,000	$ 10,000	$231,525	$ 13,892	$176,400	$ 10,584	$ 221,550	$ 13,293	$ 279,850	$ 16,791			$ 909,325	$ 181,865
(after asset purchase)																	
6	$ 74,560	$ 50,000	$ 10,000	$ 10,000	$ 10,000	$243,101	$ 14,586	$185,220	$ 11,113	$ 232,628	$ 13,958	$ 293,843	$ 17,631	$ 372,798	$ 22,368	$ 1,327,599	$ 265,518
(after asset purchase)																	

*PYF income is determined by adding contribution amount to asset income amount(s)

157

Investment Blueprint

Aggressive Stock Market

Assumptions:

Income (after tax): $ 100,000 (no consumer debt)

Net ROI on Asset: 20%

Downpmt on Asset: 100% (margin)

Asset appreciation rate: 5%

end of Year	Bank Accounts 20% PYF*	50% Livg XP	10% Education	10% Fun	10% Tithe/NE	Asset Accounts 1st Asset Value	1st Asset Income	2nd Asset Value	2nd Asset Income	3rd Asset Value	3rd Asset Income	4th Asset Value	4th Asset Income	5th Asset Value	5th Asset Income	Summary Assets Controlled	Net Worth
1	$ 20,000	$ 50,000	$ 10,000	$ 10,000	$ 10,000											$ 20,000	$ 20,000
2	$ 40,000	$ 50,000	$ 10,000	$ 10,000	$ 10,000											$ 40,000	$ 40,000
(after asset purchase) 2						$ 40,000	$ 8,000										
3	$ 28,000	$ 50,000	$ 10,000	$ 10,000	$ 10,000											$ 70,000	$ 70,000
(after asset purchase) 3						$ 42,000	$ 8,400	$ 28,000	$ 5,600								
4	$ 34,000	$ 50,000	$ 10,000	$ 10,000	$ 10,000											$ 107,500	$ 107,500
(after asset purchase) 4						$ 44,100	$ 8,820	$ 29,400	$ 5,880	$ 34,000	$ 6,800						
5	$ 41,500	$ 50,000	$ 10,000	$ 10,000	$ 10,000											$ 154,375	$ 154,375
(after asset purchase) 5						$ 46,305	$ 9,261	$ 30,870	$ 6,174	$ 35,700	$ 7,140	$ 41,500	$ 8,300				
6	$ 50,875	$ 50,000	$ 10,000	$ 10,000	$ 10,000											$ 212,969	$ 212,969
(after asset purchase) 6						$ 48,620	$ 9,724	$ 32,414	$ 6,483	$ 37,485	$ 7,497	$ 43,575	$ 8,715	$ 50,875	$ 10,175		

*PYF income is determined by adding contribution amount to asset income amount(s)

158

Investment Blueprint

Aggressive Stock Market

Assumptions:

Income (after tax): **$ 50,000** (no consumer debt)

Net ROI on Asset: 20%

Downpmt on Asset: 100% (margin)

Asset appreciation rate: 5%

end of Year	PYF* 20%	Livg XP 50%	Education 10%	Fun 10%	Tithe/NE 10%	1st Asset Value	1st Asset Income	2nd Asset Value	2nd Asset Income	3rd Asset Value	3rd Asset Income	4th Asset Value	4th Asset Income	5th Asset Value	5th Asset Income	Assets Controlled	Net Worth
1	$ 10,000	$ 25,000	$ 5,000	$ 5,000	$ 5,000											$ 10,000	$ 10,000
2	$ 20,000	$ 25,000	$ 5,000	$ 5,000	$ 5,000											$ 20,000	$ 20,000
2 (after asset purchase)						$ 20,000	$ 4,000										
3	$ 14,000	$ 25,000	$ 5,000	$ 5,000	$ 5,000											$ 35,000	$ 35,000
3 (after asset purchase)						$ 21,000	$ 4,200	$ 14,000	$ 2,800								
4	$ 17,000	$ 25,000	$ 5,000	$ 5,000	$ 5,000											$ 53,750	$ 53,750
4 (after asset purchase)						$ 22,050	$ 4,410	$ 14,700	$ 2,940	$ 17,000	$ 3,400						
5	$ 20,750	$ 25,000	$ 5,000	$ 5,000	$ 5,000											$ 77,188	$ 77,188
5 (after asset purchase)						$ 23,153	$ 4,631	$ 15,435	$ 3,087	$ 17,850	$ 3,570	$ 20,750	$ 4,150				
6	$ 25,438	$ 25,000	$ 5,000	$ 5,000	$ 5,000											$ 106,494	$ 106,494
6 (after asset purchase)						$ 24,310	$ 4,862	$ 16,207	$ 3,241	$ 18,743	$ 3,749	$ 21,788	$ 4,358	$ 25,438	$ 5,088		

Bank Accounts | Asset Accounts | Summary

*PYF income is determined by adding contribution amount to asset income amount(s)

159

Investment Blueprint

Moderate Stock Market

Assumptions:

Income (after tax): $ 100,000 (no consumer debt)

Net ROI on Asset: 12%

Downpmt on Asset: 100% (margin)

Asset appreciation rate: 5%

	Bank Accounts					Asset Accounts										Summary	
end of Year	20% PYF*	50% Livg.XP	10% Education	10% Fun	10% Tithe/NE	1st Asset Value	1st Asset Income	2nd Asset Value	2nd Asset Income	3rd Asset Value	3rd Asset Income	4th Asset Value	4th Asset Income	5th Asset Value	5th Asset Income	Assets Controlled	Net Worth
1	$ 20,000	$ 50,000	$ 10,000	$ 10,000	$ 10,000											$ 20,000	$ 20,000
2	$ 40,000	$ 50,000	$ 10,000	$ 10,000	$ 10,000											$ 40,000	$ 40,000
2 (after asset purchase)						$ 40,000	$ 4,800										
3	$ 24,800	$ 50,000	$ 10,000	$ 10,000	$ 10,000											$ 66,800	$ 66,800
3 (after asset purchase)						$ 42,000	$ 5,040	$ 24,800	$ 2,976								
4	$ 28,016	$ 50,000	$ 10,000	$ 10,000	$ 10,000											$ 98,156	$ 98,156
4 (after asset purchase)						$ 44,100	$ 5,292	$ 26,040	$ 3,125	$ 28,016	$ 3,362						
5	$ 31,779	$ 50,000	$ 10,000	$ 10,000	$ 10,000											$ 134,843	$ 134,843
5 (after asset purchase)						$ 46,305	$ 5,557	$ 27,342	$ 3,281	$ 29,417	$ 3,530	$ 31,779	$ 3,813				
6	$ 36,181	$ 50,000	$ 10,000	$ 10,000	$ 10,000											$ 177,766	$ 177,766
6 (after asset purchase)						$ 48,620	$ 5,834	$ 28,709	$ 3,445	$ 30,888	$ 3,707	$ 33,368	$ 4,004	$ 36,181	$ 4,342		

*PYF income is determined by adding contribution amount to asset income amount(s)

160

Investment Blueprint

Moderate Stock Market

Assumptions:

Income (after tax): $ 50,000 (no consumer debt)

Net ROI on Asset: 12%

Downpmt on Asset: 100% (margin)

Asset appreciation rate: 5%

end of Year	20% PYF*	50% Livg XP	10% Education	10% Fun	10% Tithe/NE	1st Asset Value	1st Asset Income	2nd Asset Value	2nd Asset Income	3rd Asset Value	3rd Asset Income	4th Asset Value	4th Asset Income	5th Asset Value	5th Asset Income	Assets Controlled	Net Worth
		Bank Accounts							*Asset Accounts*							*Summary*	
1	$ 10,000	$ 25,000	$ 5,000	$ 5,000	$ 5,000											$ 10,000	$ 10,000
2	$ 20,000	$ 25,000	$ 5,000	$ 5,000	$ 5,000											$ 20,000	$ 20,000
2 (after asset purchase)						$ 20,000	$ 2,400										
3	$ 12,400	$ 25,000	$ 5,000	$ 5,000	$ 5,000	$ 21,000	$ 2,520									$ 33,400	$ 33,400
3 (after asset purchase)								$ 12,400	$ 1,488								
4	$ 14,008	$ 25,000	$ 5,000	$ 5,000	$ 5,000	$ 22,050	$ 2,646	$ 13,020	$ 1,562							$ 49,078	$ 49,078
4 (after asset purchase)										$ 14,008	$ 1,681						
5	$ 15,889	$ 25,000	$ 5,000	$ 5,000	$ 5,000	$ 23,153	$ 2,778	$ 13,671	$ 1,641	$ 14,708	$ 1,765					$ 67,421	$ 67,421
5 (after asset purchase)												$ 15,889	$ 1,907				
6	$ 18,091	$ 25,000	$ 5,000	$ 5,000	$ 5,000	$ 24,310	$ 2,917	$ 14,355	$ 1,723	$ 15,444	$ 1,853	$ 16,684	$ 2,002	$ 18,091	$ 2,171	$ 88,883	$ 88,883
6 (after asset purchase)																	

*PYF income is determined by adding contribution amount to asset income amount(s)

Investment Blueprint

Conservative Stock Market

Assumptions:

Income (after tax): $ 50,000 (no consumer debt)
Net ROI on Asset: 8%
Downpmt on Asset: 100% (margin)
Asset appreciation rate: 5%

	20%	50%	10%	10%	10%	1st Asset	1st Asset	2nd Asset	2nd Asset	3rd Asset	3rd Asset	4th Asset	4th Asset	5th Asset	5th Asset	Assets	Net
end of Year	PYF*	Livg XP	Education	Fun	Tithe/NIE	Value	Income	Value	Income	Value	Income	Value	Income	Value	Income	Controlled	Worth
1	$ 10,000	$ 25,000	$ 5,000	$ 5,000	$ 5,000											$ 10,000	$ 10,000
2	$ 20,000	$ 25,000	$ 5,000	$ 5,000	$ 5,000											$ 20,000	$ 20,000
2 (after asset purchase)						$ 20,000	$ 1,600										
3	$ 11,600	$ 25,000	$ 5,000	$ 5,000	$ 5,000												
3 (after asset purchase)						$ 21,000	$ 1,680	$ 11,600	$ 928							$ 32,600	$ 32,600
4	$ 12,608	$ 25,000	$ 5,000	$ 5,000	$ 5,000												
4 (after asset purchase)						$ 22,050	$ 1,764	$ 12,180	$ 974	$ 12,608	$ 1,009					$ 46,838	$ 46,838
5	$ 13,747	$ 25,000	$ 5,000	$ 5,000	$ 5,000												
5 (after asset purchase)						$ 23,153	$ 1,852	$ 12,789	$ 1,023	$ 13,238	$ 1,059	$ 13,747	$ 1,100			$ 62,927	$ 62,927
6	$ 15,034	$ 25,000	$ 5,000	$ 5,000	$ 5,000												
6 (after asset purchase)						$ 24,310	$ 1,945	$ 13,428	$ 1,074	$ 13,900	$ 1,112	$ 14,434	$ 1,155	$ 15,034	$ 1,203	$ 81,107	$ 81,107

Bank Accounts — Asset Accounts — Summary

*PYF income is determined by adding contribution amount to asset income amount(s)

162

Investment Blueprint

Conservative Stock Market

Assumptions:

Income (after tax): $ 100,000 (no consumer debt)

Net ROI on Asset: 8%

Downpmt on Asset: 100% (margin)

Asset appreciation rate: 5%

end of Year	20% PYF*	50% Livg XP	10% Education	10% Fun	10% Tithe/NE	1st Asset Value	1st Asset Income	2nd Asset Value	2nd Asset Income	3rd Asset Value	3rd Asset Income	4th Asset Value	4th Asset Income	5th Asset Value	5th Asset Income	Assets Controlled	Net Worth
1	$ 20,000	$ 50,000	$ 10,000	$ 10,000	$ 10,000											$ 20,000	$ 20,000
2	$ 40,000	$ 50,000	$ 10,000	$ 10,000	$ 10,000											$ 40,000	$ 40,000
2 (after asset purchase)						$ 40,000	$ 3,200										
3	$ 23,200	$ 50,000	$ 10,000	$ 10,000	$ 10,000											$ 65,200	$ 65,200
3 (after asset purchase)						$ 42,000	3,360	$ 23,200	$ 1,856								
4	$ 25,216	$ 50,000	$ 10,000	$ 10,000	$ 10,000											$ 93,676	$ 93,676
4 (after asset purchase)						$ 44,100	3,528	$ 24,360	1,949	$ 25,216	2,017						
5	$ 27,494	$ 50,000	$ 10,000	$ 10,000	$ 10,000											$ 125,854	$ 125,854
5 (after asset purchase)						$ 46,305	3,704	$ 25,578	2,046	$ 26,477	2,118	$ 27,494	2,200				
6	$ 30,068	$ 50,000	$ 10,000	$ 10,000	$ 10,000											$ 162,215	$ 162,215
6 (after asset purchase)						$ 48,620	3,890	$ 26,857	2,149	$ 27,801	2,224	$ 28,869	2,310	$ 30,068	$ 2,405		

*PYF income is determined by adding contribution amount to asset income amount(s)

163

Investment Blueprint

Ultra Aggressive Stock Market

Assumptions:

Income (after tax): $ 100,000 (no consumer debt)

Net ROI on Asset: 40%

Downpmt on Asset: 100% (margin)

Asset appreciation rate: 5%

	end of Year	20% PYF*	50% Live XP	10% Education	10% Fun	10% Tithe/NE	1st Asset Value	1st Asset Income	2nd Asset Value	2nd Asset Income	3rd Asset Value	3rd Asset Income	4th Asset Value	4th Asset Income	5th Asset Value	5th Asset Income	Assets Controlled	Net Worth
	1	$ 20,000	$ 50,000	$ 10,000	$ 10,000	$ 10,000											$ 20,000	$ 20,000
	2	$ 40,000	$ 50,000	$ 10,000	$ 10,000	$ 10,000											$ 40,000	$ 40,000
(after asset purchase)	2						$ 40,000	$ 16,000										
	3	$ 36,000	$ 50,000	$ 10,000	$ 10,000	$ 10,000	$ 42,000	$ 16,800									$ 78,000	$ 78,000
(after asset purchase)	3								$ 36,000	$ 14,400								
	4	$ 51,200	$ 50,000	$ 10,000	$ 10,000	$ 10,000	$ 44,100	$ 17,640	$ 37,800	$ 15,120							$ 133,100	$ 133,100
(after asset purchase)	4										$ 51,200	$ 20,480						
	5	$ 73,240	$ 50,000	$ 10,000	$ 10,000	$ 10,000	$ 46,305	$ 18,522	$ 39,690	$ 15,876	$ 53,760	$ 21,504					$ 212,995	$ 212,995
(after asset purchase)	5												$ 73,240	$ 29,296				
	6	$ 105,198	$ 50,000	$ 10,000	$ 10,000	$ 10,000	$ 48,620	$ 19,448	$ 41,675	$ 16,670	$ 56,448	$ 22,579	$ 76,902	$ 30,761	$ 105,198	$ 42,079	$ 328,843	$ 328,843
(after asset purchase)	6																	

*PYF income is determined by adding contribution amount to asset income amount(s)

164

CONCLUSION

CONCLUSION

So here you are. You've got the basics. You've got the formula. It works, but it is going to take discipline. And you can do it. You've learned about passive income, your home, income, spending, investment vehicles and powerful concepts like compounding interest. It is simple, but it isn't always easy, but it is very do-able.

So, are you going to do it?

If so, go back through your notes and make some decisions RIGHT NOW and decide what is your first step. Then, schedule it. Because if you don't schedule your first action item, you just may never get around to it. But if you do schedule it, you can start to get momentum.

Like compounding interest, it is the small things that you do early that accumulate into success over time. So do it! Do it now! What are you going to schedule?

_____

_____

Remember to download your bonuses at:

http://www.HackingMoney.com/bonuses

Good luck and thank you for sharing your success with the world!

NEXT STEPS

So, I hope that this is not the end for you and me. We have so many ways to help that are simple and affordable, but can help you springboard your life to even greater success.

You see, I come from the belief that **we just don't learn the right stuff in our schools**. Sure, we understand isosceles triangles and the Pythagorean Theorem. We learn about Henry the 8th and his headless wives. We study Cleopatra and Romeo and Juliet.

That's all great, but we don't learn much of the things that we need in life, things that make it easy to be successful in the world. Imagine if our schools taught us these things:
- Time Management and Goal-setting
- Communications skills
- Relationship skills
- Intimacy Skills
- Money skills
- Leadership Skills
- Nutrition and fitness skills
- Negotiating Skills
- Basic Business Skills

Wouldn't our lives be easier if they taught these things to us? Well, they didn't, did they? So we have created a curriculum that covers these topics and gives you the tools that you need to succeed in life.

You can find out more at:
www.HackingMoney.com/school

If you found this book valuable, I have a special deal for you, for a limited time. I have created a course called The Hacking Money Investing System which takes everything that you learned in this book and applies it by teaching you step by step exactly how to take your financial life to the next level. The Course covers the following in depth:

- All the financial instruments with illustrations and examples
- Video instructions of how to apply the knowledge
- Quizzes and tests to ensure that you are retaining the concepts
- The 5 Financial Building Blocks applied
- The Earnings Allocation Formula applied
- A community to hold you accountable and provide support

As a reader of this book, you are entitled to a special deal on the course. I have provided all of the details here:

http://www.HackingMoney.com/courseoffer

THANK YOU FOR READING

I hope you enjoyed this CourseBook. I really appreciate your feedback, and I love hearing what you have to say, because we can always learn and get better.

Could you please leave me a review on Amazon letting me know what you thought of the course?

Thank you so much! If you want to get in touch, come find me in my corner of the internet:

http://www.MarkYegge.com

Other titles by Mark Yegge:

Negotiate To Win-Win (NegotiateToWinWin.com);

The Secrets of Business (TheSecretsOfBusiness.com)

Investing Basics: (DestinyCreation.com/InvestingBasics)

Hedge Fund Investing Secrets.com

Hedge Fund Investing Strategies.com

Jump Start your Financial Life

The 7 Secrets of Trading

10 Ways To 10X Your Life

Other books on Amazon:

Negotiate to Win Win (Audible Version Available)

The Secrets of Business

SPECIAL LINKS FOR YOU AS A READER OF THIS BOOK:

https://www.HackingMoney.com/blueprint

https://www.HackingMoney.com/spreadsheet

https://www.HackingMoney.com/BONUSES

https://www.HackingMoney.com/school

http://www.HackingMoney.com/courseoffer

RESOURCES

RESOURCES

Below is a list of links and useful sites that I've referenced throughout the book, and others, that you will find useful and easy to refer back to as you are employing the subjects covered in this course work.

- http://www.IRS.gov
- https://thecollegeinvestor.com/resources/
- https://thecollegeinvestor.com/16399/20-passive-income-ideas/
- https://www.investopedia.com/terms/c/compoundinterest.asp
- https://www.investor.gov/additional-resources/free-financial-planning-tools/compound-interest-calculator
- https://en.wikipedia.org/wiki/Inflation
- https://www.vcita.com/blog/author/laura-mcarthur
- https://www.investopedia.com/terms/a/assetallocation.asp
- https://tools.finra.org/retirement_calculator/

ABOUT THE AUTHOR

Mark Yegge has spent his entire life learning and teaching people about wealth and personal development. He started his first business when he was 10 years old and invested the profits in stocks when he was 12 – and made enough to buy his first car.

He sold his Wall Street software company and retired at the age of 39, but not before growing the company from $0 to a $30-million dollar enterprise as its CEO. Along the way, he and his company garnered awards such as: Small Business of the Year, the Florida 100, and the Fast 500 – recognizing the fastest-growing companies in America.

Personally, he was recognized twice by Ernst and Young as an Entrepreneur of the Year finalist.

Today, he manages a hedge fund and provides financial advice and business and financial education through:
- DestinyCreation.com,
- HackingMoney.com,
- StockTradeGenius.com
- and seminars throughout North America.

He speaks to audiences about business, wealth management, and personal development and has been recognized as one of the top worldwide trainers with the

Dale Carnegie Organization where he helps people become excellent public speakers and business leaders.

www.ingramcontent.com/pod-product-compliance
Lightning Source LLC
Chambersburg PA
CBHW021929190326
41519CB00009B/959